Sports in Cleveland

The Encyclopedia of Cleveland History: Illustrated Volumes
Edited by David D. Van Tassel and John J. Grabowski

1. *Cleveland: A Concise History, 1796–1990*, by Carol Poh Miller and Robert Wheeler
2. *Sports in Cleveland: An Illustrated History*, by John J. Grabowski

Sports in Cleveland

AN ILLUSTRATED HISTORY

John J.
Grabowski

*An
Encyclopedia of
Cleveland History
Project*

*Indiana
University
Press*

BLOOMINGTON
AND INDIANAPOLIS

Library of Congress Cataloging-in-Publication Data

Grabowski, John J.
    Sports in Cleveland : an illustrated history / John J. Grabowski.
        p.   cm.—(The encyclopedia of Cleveland history ; 2)
    Includes index.
    ISBN 0-253-32620-6 (alk. paper).—ISBN 0-253-20747-9 (pbk. :
alk. paper)
    1. Sports—Ohio—Cleveland—History.   2. Cleveland (Ohio)—Social
conditions.   I. Title.   II. Series.
GV584.5.C58G73   1992
796′ .09771′32—dc20   92-7904

1 2 3 4 5 96 95 94 93 92

Contents

EDITORS' PREFACE

When we were editing the *Encyclopedia of Cleveland History*, we decided to illustrate the volume with a limited number of charts and maps. This decision was made in order to preserve space for articles on the many institutions, events, and people who played an important role in the development of the city and who deserved to be included. However, we were conscious that we were missing a form of documentation that has become very important in today's world. Cleveland has an extremely rich store of photographic archives, from the 250,000 images in the library of the Western Reserve Historical Society to the extensive *Cleveland Press* Collection held at the Cleveland State University Library, to the extraordinary Cleveland Picture Collection at the Cleveland Public Library. We hope, therefore, to offer a series of illustrated volumes drawing on these collections and focusing on particular aspects of Cleveland's history, from sports and the fine arts to industry and business, as well as many things in between.

Sports in Cleveland: An Illustrated History follows the earlier publication of *Cleveland: A Concise History, 1796–1990* as the second volume in the projected series of illustrated histories. It is appropriate that this should be the first book on a specialized aspect of the history of the city of Cleveland because sports has long been an integral and highly visible part of the life of the community. In addition, this is the first such overview of the development of the whole panoply of sports in the context of a particular city.

John Grabowski has produced not only an up-to-date, accurate, and brief history, but also a new synthesis and interpretation which should enable the reader to understand the role of sports in the development of Cleveland, as well as how a particular sport became part of the fabric of the city's life. This volume explains how recreational sports merged into professional sports teams, how some games such as golf and tennis were introduced into the community as activities of the wealthy and were gradually democratized. It also tells the story of how particular team sports became central to the city's economy and symbolic of its well-being.

We have carefully selected photographs and illustrations to support the text. Wherever possible we have chosen images never before published. These illustrations are designed to evoke the flavor and the character of the time, as well as to furnish a visual image of outstanding athletes, promoters, events, and arenas.

Although John Grabowski has written his own acknowledgments, we, as editors, owe a debt of thanks to many people and institutions. Thanks first and foremost to the Cleveland Foundation, which has come forth with funding that helped make possible this along with other volumes in the project. In addition, we would like to thank the Cleveland Indians Baseball Company and the Cleveland Browns, who furnished funding essential to the completion of this volume. The editors appreciate the work of Sarah Snock, who served not only as project coordinator but also did some of the photographic research, and Michael Morgenstern, who served as research assistant, checked and condensed much of the information, researched through many photographic collections, and wrote captions. Mary Stavish also did important research for the volume, and Michael

McCormick did the photographic copy work. We would especially like to thank the wonderful group of editorial advisors: Del Bethel, August "Augie" Bossu, Robert Dolgan, Robert Gries, Frances Kaszubski, Robert Malaga, and Maralyn West, who met a number of times and provided many good suggestions for the improvement of this volume.

David D. Van Tassel
Case Western Reserve University

John J. Grabowski
Western Reserve Historical Society

PREFACE

Like many of the sports it discusses, this volume is a product of team effort. As its author, I am indebted first and foremost to David D. Van Tassel for creating the *Encyclopedia of Cleveland History* illustrated series and for considering me as qualified to prepare the text. As a student of urban history with specialization in the fields of immigration and ethnicity, I approach sports as a subject that is neither alien to me nor an area of expertise. The faith of the general editor in my ability is therefore much appreciated, and I hope that it is justified.

The work of several authors who contributed to the original *Encyclopedia of Cleveland History* was critical to my own work. Essays in that volume by Michael McCormick, Craig Miller, Kenneth Rose, Fred Schuld, Mary Stavish, and Edward E. Worthington provided both a factual framework for this volume and suggestions for the interpretive path I selected. The assistance, advice, and constructive criticism on the part of the volume's advisory committee helped me further develop my interpretation of sports in Cleveland and, importantly, helped me avoid a number of factual "errors." Those errors that certainly will find their way to the scorecard are, of course, fully attributable to the author.

Very special acknowledgment is due to the staff of the Encyclopedia office. Sarah Snock and Michael Morgenstern spent countless hours seeking illustrations for the volume, preparing captions, and overseeing a multitude of technical details. Michael McCormick is responsible for the excellent reproductions that are contained herein. Mary Stavish deserves particular praise for voluntarily enlisting in the project to research and write a number of the boxed captions used throughout the book. My wife, Diane Ewart Grabowski, served as an editor with an eye to both style and clarity. Our ongoing dialectic about this project was invaluable and helped me avoid several interpretive pitfalls.

Finally, if this work shows any sensitivity to the meaning sports has had for large numbers of people, it derives not from my historical training or any time I have spent on the playing fields but from the experience of my two fathers. It is to them, Ben Grabowski and David Ewart, that I owe my greatest debt for showing me that in sports, feeling is as important as fact.

INTRODUCTION

During the early months of 1991, Clevelanders, like most Americans, spent anxious hours watching television reports of the war in the Persian Gulf and reviewing the Middle Eastern situation in their daily newspaper. From mid-January until early March, the Gulf Crisis dominated the news and daily conversation. Only once did war really slip from the headlines—that being the week of February 4, when the Cleveland Browns football team hired a new head coach, Bill Belichick. Not even coverage of the season's Super Bowl on January 27 had broken the local spell of the war, but the fate of the Browns was something else, a matter of great local import. What the Cleveland Browns achieved as a team was, to Clevelanders of the 1990s, inextricably linked not only to the city's reputation but to its economic and civic well-being as well.

How had a sport, indeed sports generally, become such an all-encompassing matter, so that the life-and-death issues of war were subordinate to it? Humans have played games throughout recorded history, but for much of that time those games were minor diversions in lives occupied with the struggle and routine of supplying the necessities of life. Play, usually associated with children, perhaps became an adult diversion when activities central to providing sustenance became competitive. Hunting scenes in neolithic caves may or may not represent activity based on need. We do know, however, that archery contests, wrestling, and other activities related to physical prowess did assume the stature of contests in ancient Egypt. Minoan civilization placed similar emphasis on contests. It remained for the Greeks, however, to formalize and immortalize such activities with the creation of the Olympics, first recorded in 776 B.C. Beginning with a simple footrace, the Olympics eventually encompassed other events, the discus, javelin, and wrestling, for example. All of these, however, measured prowess in a civilization accustomed to battles and warefare—pretechnological warfare powered by the bodies of men.

The Romans continued the tradition of the Greeks, but with major differences. Whereas the Greek Olympics were contests held to find a particular champion, the Roman games were staged for the benefit of the crowd. Some historians have speculated that the Greeks fostered a tradition of amateur sport, while the Romans worked on a professional model. Juvenal well knew the purpose of Roman sport when he posited his now famous maxim "Duas tantum res anxius optat, Panem et circenses" [The people long eagerly for two things—bread and circuses].

The blood and savagery associated with Roman sport guaranteed its decline during the Christian era. People continued to play games, however. Most often these were contests involving the movement of a ball to a goal. This type of activity could be found in Aztec and Mayan civilization, as well as in ancient Chinese and Japanese life. In Japan, the ritual performance was known as *kemari*. The ball games played in medieval Europe eventually provided the basis for modern rugby, soccer, and American football. Contests associated with physical prowess continued, of course, in such guises as the archery and jousting tournaments of the Middle Ages, and Celtic contests that measured an ability to hurl rocks and other missiles the greatest distance. The Scottish games performed annually in many parts of the world today derive from such tests of warlike skills.

Sports as we know them today—organized contests with measurable results—trace their origins to England in the late seventeenth century. The cricket, handicapped horseracing, and regulated boxing contests that developed during the period of the Enlightenment grew into the rationalized competitive activities that have become so much a part of late-twentieth-century life. The founding of the Marylebone Cricket Club in 1787 can be viewed as the final step in a development in which simple play evolved to a level of organized play and then to competitive games (contests), and finally to physical contests or sports as we have come to know them.

In the year the Marylebone Cricket Club was formed, the area now known as Greater Cleveland was a largely uninhabited wilderness. Indeed, in that year two Moravian missionaries, David Zeisberger and John Heckewelder, decided to abandon what had been the initial attempt to create a settlement, an Indian mission known as Pilgerruh, which had been built along the Cuyahoga River in what is now Valley View, Ohio. It is probable that no organized games were played at Pilgerruh.

Some nine years later, when the surveyors of the Connecticut Land Company led by Moses Cleaveland again brought European civilization to the area, there was no time for games and no space in their packs for the implements of play. Cleaveland and his surveying party, along with the meager number of settlers who would follow in the next two decades, were not interested in games—they were absorbed by the process of making a living, indeed surviving, in a harsh environment. As the settlement they established at last began to grow in the 1820s and 1830s, some of its inhabitants began to accumulate the wealth and leisure time necessary for the pursuit of play and, later, organized sports. By the end of the century, the city was a wealthy metropolis of over 300,000 people, and organized sport in the form of baseball, basketball, football, track and field, and a variety of other group and individual endeavors formed an important part of local life. However, the significance of such activity was minor in terms of economic impact. The city's leadership saw its future in terms of industrial output, and not in the services associated with leisure activities. The performance of local teams, however, was increasingly viewed as a part of the city's public image.

As the turn of another century nears, all has changed. In 1990s Cleveland, sports are no longer a leisure-time activity but a multimillion-dollar business that has come to dominate the local economy in a way that could never have been envisioned by the community's leadership a hundred years ago, let alone by its founders. Moreover, the performance of local teams has become central to the area's self-esteem. Perhaps most critical, the players on those teams have become role models whose achievements have great meaning for the many racial and nationality communities that make up the city.

This transformation of the role of sports in the life of Cleveland and its citizens is the focus of this volume. What is important to the history of sports in Cleveland is not only the win-loss records of its teams or the statistics of and anecdotes about the great and near-great who have played on the city's fields; what is important is the way in which "organized play" has become woven into the fabric of civic life and to what degree, if any, Cleveland has differed from the rest of the country in establishing its sports culture. In this review of the growth of sports, attention will be focused on the major team sports, including baseball, basketball, hockey, and football, and individual participatory sports such as horseracing, tennis, golf, boxing, track and field, and bowling. Auto racing and other mechanized endeavors, including aircraft racing, will find mention in the text but will not be dealt with in any detail, nor will a variety of minor individual sports such as swimming, squash, and fencing. What follows is a history of the enormous change brought about by sports in Cleveland, a change that has reshaped the local economy, provided individual and group opportunity, and, most important, created a mirror in which the psyche of the city has been reflected.

Sports in Cleveland

Sport in the Preindustrial City, 1796–1865

The year 1820 saw the publication of what may have been the first general sports book in the United States, *Children's Amusements: When School Is Over for the Day, the Sprightly Boys Run Off to Play*. The volume detailed a number of games and activities, including cricket, archery, and skating, that it found suitable for youth. It is doubtful that any children in the village of Cleveland had access to the book, and if they had, whether they would have taken up the games it described is equally questionable.

Sports and games had little place in the struggling community. During the first three decades following its founding in 1796, Cleveland seemed a hopeless proposition. Settlers struggled through the wilderness to the banks of the Cuyahoga, but many soon left the malarial confines of the slow-flowing river. Those who did manage to stay, both farmers and would-be merchants, awaited the fulfillment of the economic promise the area's founders had seen in the site where a great river joined Lake Erie. Those who persisted—the settlement had a population of 87 in 1810 and 606 in 1820—were probably too busy with survival in a rough wilderness to devote time to games. Their children undoubtedly did play, and it is likely that the first sports practiced in Cleveland were swimming and impromptu races and wrestling matches among the settlement's younger inhabitants.

Leisure time for the area's adult settlers was almost nonexistent. Even the traditional day of rest on the Sabbath was lost during the region's first two decades. Until the 1820s, Clevelanders had a reputation for being irreligious, preferring to devote Sunday to work rather than to worship. When religion did arrive, honoring the Sabbath became standard for the largely Protestant community, a custom that excluded all but the most subtle and religiously oriented recreation on the day of the Lord. It would take many decades for the Sabbatarian laws to be relaxed, and this would have great impact on how and when Clevelanders would eventually enjoy their sports and recreational pursuits.

What recreation adults did pursue during this time centered about activities that mirrored the needs of the frontier community and the skills requisite for survival on the edge of civilization. Group hunting was one such activity. In 1819, for example, 300 men gathered in the woods in Chagrin (Willoughby) during the Christmas season and managed to bag two elk, seventy-five deer, twenty-three bears, seventeen wolves, and ten turkeys. A similar mass hunt had been held in Hinckley in 1818 with even greater success, but its purposes were less recreational—settlers were still recovering from 1816, known as the "year without a summer," and with the failure of regional crops, it was incumbent upon them to fill their larders in any way they could.

Eventually, such frontier sports would become more organized within the institution of the county fair, where they would be joined by other contests built around agricultural activities. A regional fair held in Warren in 1822, for instance, featured a plowing match. These fairs were modeled after the Berkshire, Massachusetts, County Fair, which began in 1810. The first Cuyahoga County Fair was held in Cleveland, on Public Square, in 1829, some six years after the residents of Geauga County had held their first fair. At these events people measured not only their agricultural and domestic accomplishments through the exhibition of livestock, produce, and domestic products, but also their skills at woodchopping, running, wrestling, and marksmanship. Turkey shoots were, indeed, contests, but ones that measured a critical frontier skill. Visitors to today's county fairs will find many of the same contests, none of which, however, are set against the background of necessity experienced by their ancestors.

The dependence of Clevelanders on frontier skills would disappear with the coming of the Ohio and Erie Canal in the late 1820s. Connecting Cleveland first with Akron (1827) and eventually with Portsmouth on the Ohio River (1832), the canal would fulfill the vision of the community's founders and transform the struggling settlement into a thriving mercantile center. By 1830 Cleveland's population had risen to 1,075. Ten years later it stood at 6,071. By 1860, over 40,000 people lived in the city. More important than population growth, however, was the prosperity enjoyed by successful city merchants, and the leisure time surplus wealth began, at last, to create.

In terms of sports, the most immediate manifestation of a thriving community was the beginning of horseracing. The "sport of kings" had entered an organized phase in Great Britain in the seventeenth century. By the 1830s, racetracks with grandstands began to be built in major eastern United States cities. In Cleveland, racing probably began with casual match races. This was not an activity engaged in by many citizens, including the area's farmers, whose draft animals were likely to be oxen or, at best, heavy work horses. Rather, it was the merchant, lawyer, or other professional member of the citizenry who would enter into such a challenge. One of the earliest reports of a match race in Cleveland described a contest held on Erie (East 9th) Street which took the participants from St. Clair to Huron Street.

By 1850, local prosperity allowed for the creation of the Cleveland Jockey Club, which sponsored both pacing and trotting contests during an annual five-day meet. These were likely held on the Forest City Course, which had been built between what is now East 9th and East 14th streets. As the city expanded in the ensuing years, new courses were built farther from its center at sites on Fremont Street (now Lansing Avenue), at the Richards Hotel at what is now East 89th and Euclid Avenue, and on the grounds of the various county fairs. Eventually, the fairground constructed in Glenville became the site of the city's most illustrious nineteenth-century track.

As formal racing developed, the cost of buying and maintaining a fine competi-

tive animal ruled out participation for many Cleveland residents. The sport therefore developed an éclat unlike that enjoyed by any other sporting activity in the city's history, save polo, which, of course, depended on fine horseflesh as well.

There was as much pleasure in showing one's animal as in racing it, and by the 1850s, events for show became common, particularly as horses were available to the more prosperous area farmers. In early 1856 an informal challenge by Solon residents resulted in what can only be termed a sleighing meet for show as towns and then counties vied with one another to see which could turn out the most "cutters." The Solonites started the challenge by mounting a force of seven four-horse cutters. By mid-March, the challenge ended with Medina County turning out 185 sleighs at a single time.

The 1850s were an important decade in local sports history, for by this time the city of Cleveland was large and prosperous enough to offer a variety of diversions to its citizens. Few of these new sporting activities centered about large-scale, organized play. Most catered to individual needs and pocketbooks. Harsh local winters could now, for instance, be used to advantage by those with money for a pair of ice skates. Presumably, the Scots in Cleveland's increasingly diverse population were the ones who instituted curling, a wintertime activity first reported in the 1850s and which still continued in the 1990s in the confines of the Cleveland Skating Club.

As railroads and telegraph wires forged connections with other parts of the United States, Clevelanders began to partake in new national sporting trends. Organized competitive rowing began in Cleveland in 1855 with the formation of the Ivanhoe Boat Club. The club raced other groups, including a team from Sandusky, on the Cuyahoga River for several years. Eventually, commercial traffic on the river prevented further contests. In creating a rowing club, Clevelanders were following a national trend that was, in turn, based on admiration for the rowing meets between major British universities. The first such major American match, between teams from Yale and Harvard, occurred only three years before the Ivanhoe Club's first race. The less athletically demanding game of billiards also appeared in Cleveland in the 1850s, just at the time it was beginning to enjoy nationwide popularity. By the 1860s, Clevelanders could watch set matches between national champions at venues such as Brainard's Hall, and partake of the sport themselves at locations throughout the city.

The decade preceding the Civil War also saw the establishment of the city's first gymnasium. Situated on Superior Street, Cleveland's main thoroughfare, the facility offered ladders, bars, and swinging apparatus. One can only speculate as to the clientele of this establishment—perhaps it consisted of clerks and merchants anxious to stave off the ill effects of their sedentary urban occupations. In addition to using the apparatus, those who patronized the gymnasium also watched the boxing, wresting, and running events it sponsored. After the Civil War, the activities of the gymnasium would become part of the purview of private athletic clubs and, eventually, the more egalitarian YMCA.

Almost unnoticed during the rise of individual sporting and recreational activity in Cleveland during the 1850s was the first emergence of group athletic activity. Central in almost all of the brief newspaper notices of such activity was the term *ball playing.* Somewhat belatedly, Cleveland was taking up the national pastime of baseball.

Baseball can trace its roots to the English game of rounders (which was probably played by children in Cleveland), and may have been played as early as the 1820s in New York State. Games involving a bat and ball were reportedly engaged in by Washington's troops at Valley Forge. However, the modern game derives in part from rules and field dimensions that were laid down under the guidance of Alexander Cartwright of New York City in 1845. Cartwright was one of the chief figures in the Knickerbocker team of that city. The Knickerbockers, like teams that formed in Boston, Philadelphia, Lowell, Massachusetts, Allegheny, Pennsylvania, and Hartford, Connecticut, before the Civil War, were totally amateur, their ranks often drawn from the middle-class clerks and merchants of these cities. Other teams, such as the Brooklyn Atlantics, were made up of workingmen. The membership of amateur teams often reflected neighborhoods or occupations. By 1856 baseball was well enough advanced along the eastern seaboard to be termed "The American National Game of Base Ball" in a *Spirit of the Times* headline.

How and when baseball came to Cleveland in any real organized fashion is still to be determined. Cricket may have come to the city first; the St. George Cricket Club played here in the early 1850s. We do know that in 1857 a "ball game" was reported on Public Square, and that protests were raised against the use of the square for a pastime that was beginning to acquire a less than upper-class reputation. Similar ball games played by children were a feature of some of the city's Fourth of July celebrations. These Independence Day festivities were one of the few times at which the citizenry, free from a normal work schedule, could disport itself without fear of violating Sabbatarian laws. Given the simplicity of the equipment, the availability of printed rules, and the city's good connections with East Coast news, it is probable that a number of amateur nines existed in the area before the Civil War. However, it was only after that conflict that a strong, traceable, organized form of the sport emerged here.

During the brief thirty-five-year period from the commencement of canal construction to the eve of the American Civil War, Cleveland had evolved from an economic backwater into a community of 43,417 people engaged in a variety of commercial and industrial endeavors. These enterprises, in addition to attracting a large and ethnically diverse population, had made possible the accumulation of wealth and leisure time for certain of the citizenry. That time and wealth, in turn, allowed Cleveland to add sports to its growing spectrum of social and civic activities. In the next six decades, the city's wealth would grow beyond the dreams of its founders and make possible a huge expansion of sports and leisure-time activities that would involve all segments of the citizenry and become, itself, part of the expanding local economy.

Teams, Time, and Money: Nascent Modern Sports in Cleveland, 1860–1920

In the six decades from the end of the Civil War to the end of World War I, Cleveland changed more drastically than at any other time in its history. Its population burgeoned to 796,841, making it, in 1920, the nation's fifth-largest city. The diversity of the population, which included more than fifty ethnic groups, would have been unfathomable to the city's New England founders. On the edge of industrialism in 1860, Cleveland was by 1920 one of the nation's industrial powerhouses, producing iron, steel, ships, nuts, bolts, automobiles, and a host of other products, the total value of which exceeded $1.2 billion. Vast fortunes were amassed by families named Rockefeller, Hanna, Mather, and Norton, and were made visible in the string of mansions lining Euclid Avenue, a street then termed "Millionaires' Row." Those who contributed to this prosperity through their employment in the mills, on the railroads, and on the docks did not necessarily share in it to an equitable degree, and Cleveland, like many American cities, experienced political and labor movements that attempted to redress the imbalance.

Rich or poor, however, Cleveland's citizens had an increasing need for recreation and sports in the period following the Civil War. For those of means, the proper sports provided a symbol of their status and, eventually, an investment opportunity that might further increase their wealth. For the average citizen, often laboring long hours in what was commonly a six-day work week, sports provided an arena of respite from everyday life, and the heroes of that arena served as models for advancement. Even for those newly arrived in Cleveland from countries around the world, sports were important, as they sometimes provided a means for perpetuating cultural values and achieving nationalistic goals.

Whatever meaning sports may have had for a particular citizen of Cleveland, one theme seemed to govern the games people played and watched during the late nineteenth and early twentieth centuries. Amateurism in Cleveland, as throughout the country, gave way to professionalism and organization. Casual Fourth of July

games were supplanted by teams traveling to a set schedule, by sports (such as basketball) created to meet a specific need, and by the gate and ticket taker. In a sense, sports became part of the "search for order" that historian Robert Wiebe has found to characterize American life during this period. Like American business and industry, sports were rationalized, made more efficient, and made more profitable. In no sport was this athletic search for order more apparent than in the national pastime, baseball.

Baseball seems to have hit its stride during and immediately after the Civil War. Union army units, particularly from New York, took the game with them to their barracks and bivouacs, where others unfamiliar with the game undoubtedly became aware of its pleasures and its rules. The camps and staging areas where large organized masses of men were often confined provided an ideal breeding ground for the sport. In one instance in 1862, 40,000 people watched a Civil War camp game. When the soldiers returned to their home towns, they perhaps had learned the new game and, through their military training, gained the organizational skills necessary to field a unified team and schedule regular engagements with other teams.

The first record of organized amateur baseball in Cleveland was the formation of the Forest City Club by the Forest City Baseball Association in 1865. The club's first game, against the Penfields of Oberlin, ended in a 67 to 28 loss. That game, as well as other local contests, was played on the Case Commons on Putnam (East 38th) Street between Central and Scoville avenues. By 1868, the club had 150 members and a decent record against other northern Ohio teams. During that year it played one of its first nonlocal games. Unfortunately, the June 24th match against the Athletics of Philadelphia ended in an 85 to 11 defeat.

This loss may have provided the impetus for the club to become professional. By 1869 it had 300 members, including a young Leonard Hanna (a member of what would become one of Cleveland's leading families), who played second base. How-

Baseball during the Civil War: The 48th New York Volunteer Infantry, Company H, gathers at Fort Pulaski, Ga., for a company photo in the foreground, while in the background a ballgame is in progress. *Western Reserve Historical Society.*

The FOREST CITY BASEBALL CLUB, or the Forest Citys, was the name of several early amateur and professional baseball teams in Cleveland. Originally formed in 1865, the teams playing under the Forest City name were an amalgam of amateurs and pros who enjoyed limited success on the field. On 17 Mar. 1871, the Forest Citys became a charter member of the National Association of Professional Baseball Players, though the team folded a year later. The Forest Citys were revived in the National League from 1879 to 1884, but a shortage of players in 1885 led to the club's demise.

ever, association president Peter Rose felt it necessary to hire three professional players—outfielder and first baseman Arthur Allison, pitcher Albert G. "Uncle Al" Pratt, and catcher James L. "Deacon" White—to improve the team's performance. White's pay was initially $75 per month and eventually rose to $2,100 per season. The employment of the professionals caused several amateur members of the club to resign in protest.

The hybrid Forest City Club played its first professional game on June 2, 1869, in front of 2,000 spectators, losing to the nation's first professional club, the Cincinnati Red Stockings, by a score of 25 to 6. If anything, the loss against the Cincinnati team (which enjoyed a perfect season in 1869) convinced the association of the need to completely professionalize the club. This move culminated on March 17, 1871, when the Cleveland club joined the National Association of Professional Baseball Players. This association, which represented the first move toward a national pro-

Members of the Forest City Baseball Club in the early 1880s. *Western Reserve Historical Society.*

fessional organization, was noteworthy in that it replaced an older amateur association and, more particularly, in that it was built not around the owners of teams but around the players themselves. The professionals who played the game viewed themselves as part of a cooperative rather than employees of a business, a view that would cause considerable controversy in the years to come. Of particular interest as a comparison to modern baseball is the fact that the league entry fee was a mere $10, and ticket prices were set at $.25 each! The players of Cleveland were joined by players from Rockford, Chicago, Fort Wayne, Boston, Washington, Philadelphia, New York, and Troy in creating the league.

The concept of pay for play, which attracted the best players to a limited number of clubs, all but destroyed attendance for the remaining amateur groups in the city. One of these, the Cleveland Railroad Nine (composed of local railworkers), was one of the best amateur clubs in Cleveland, having defeated the tough Brooklyn Atlantics in 1867 and 1868. Its demise was assured, however, when the Forest City team went professional. Amateur teams would continue to organize and play in cities such as Cleveland in the future, but for the remainder of the century, attention would be focused on the professional teams.

Not that professionalism seemed to help the Forest City nine. Playing at a new field at Willson (East 55th Street) and Garden (Central) Avenue, the team finished in seventh place (in a nine-team league) in 1871. By mid-season of 1872, the team record was six wins and fifteen losses, at which time it probably dropped out of the league.

For a seven-year interregnum, Cleveland had no professional baseball team. During this period baseball itself was undergoing a critical change. The establishment of the National League in 1876 signaled the beginning of the modern business phase of the game. The new league was an owners' league composed of individuals or stock companies who ran the teams. The players were now employees rather than partners. The imposition of the reserve clause by the league shortly after its creation confirmed this. The regulation required players to bind their services to a particular team. No longer could individuals move from team to team in search of better pay. Freedom was curtailed, but salaries and rosters were stabilized and profits for owners made more possible.

Stabilizing teams and cutting costs were just two of the factors behind creation of the new league; a third was improving the tone of the game. By the 1870s baseball had begun to acquire a reputation as an event that attracted beer-drinking, boisterous crowds filled with gamblers and pickpockets. The league banned beer at games, prohibited all Sunday play, discouraged the use of foul language by players and fans, and raised ticket prices to $.50 (double the then standard rate) in order to cultivate a better clientele. To even further encourage that clientele, the National League owners eventually introduced padded box seats.

Cleveland entered this new world of business baseball in 1879 with another team named the Forest Citys. The city's National League entry was organized by J. Ford Evans, who had been involved with the previous professional team, and businessman William Hollinger. The team managed three winning seasons during its six years of existence, finishing third (47–37) in 1880, fifth (42–40) in 1882, and fourth (55–42) in 1883. In 1884 it fell to seventh place in the eight-team league, finishing with a 35 and 77 record. In 1885 it withdrew from the league. If anything stands out about the record of this team, it is probably the performance of pitcher Jim McCormick, who in 1879–80 pitched a total of 136 games, winning 65 and losing 68. Equally notable, at least in terms of baseball history rather than local pride, was the fact that the Forest Citys were on the losing end of the first perfect game in organized baseball when they fell victim to John Lee Richmond of the Worcester, Massachusetts, team on June 12, 1880.

The CLEVELAND SPIDERS, owned by streetcar tycoon Frank De-Haas Robison, were a professional baseball team in Cleveland from 1887 to 1899. Playing in the American Association during the 1887–88 season, the team came over to the National League in 1888. Initially known as the Forest Citys, the club acquired the nickname "Spiders" in 1889. By 1891, the Spiders moved to Robison's League Park, and manager Pat Tebeau transformed them into a rowdy contender. They won the Temple Cup in 1895, but in 1899 Robison transferred the team's best players to his St. Louis franchise, and the Spiders folded in 1900.

Not wanting to abandon a good name, Cleveland's next professional team was also initially known as the Forest Citys. It was organized in 1887 in affiliation with the American Association, the so-called beer ball or beer and whiskey league. The association had been established in 1881 as an answer to the owner-dominated National League. Originally, the association promised its players that it would not impose a reserve clause, but a later "National Agreement" with the National League overrode that. What the new league did hold onto, however, was a commitment to less formality at the ballpark. It did allow beer at its games, and, more important, it scheduled contests on Sundays, which allowed more working people to enjoy the game and increased gate receipts for the owners.

The principals in the establishment of Cleveland's newest team were owner Frank DeHaas Robison, a street railway magnate, and secretary George W. Howe (a

The Cleveland Spiders in the mid-1890s. *National Baseball Library, Coopers-town, New York.*

Cleveland Mayor Tom L. Johnson throws out the first ball at the new Brookside Park diamond, ca. 1905. *Western Reserve Historical Society.*

nephew of Elias Howe, inventor of the sewing machine). Robison was a shrewd businessman and realized that the workers of the growing industrial city of Cleveland (by the mid-1880s, the city's population exceeded 160,000 people) would patronize Sunday baseball. To further ensure his own profits, he built a new ballpark on his streetcar line at Payne Avenue and East 39th Street (the previous Forest City club had played at Kennard [East 46th] Street and Cedar). Sunday games may have proved profitable, but they did bring legal charges against the team for violation of blue laws, as well as impose a rigorous travel schedule on the Cleveland nine and its competitors. Teams made a special effort to travel to cities where Sunday ball was not strictly challenged, and then to return to their home fields by the early weekdays.

In 1889, the team moved to the National League and acquired a new name, the Cleveland Spiders, supposedly because of the "skinny and spindly" appearance of many of its players. What prompted the move to the older, established league is unknown, other than the fact that the slot occupied by the Detroit team had opened up. Possibly, Robison felt his interests would be more secure in the senior circuit. The choice was a wise one, for within three years the American Association folded, and its four remaining teams joined the National League. The tension that existed between labor and capital in the national pastime, however, found another manifestation in 1890 with the formation of the Players' National League by members of the Brotherhood of Professional Base Ball Players. The new league represented an attempt by the players to break out of the reserve restrictions and pay scales of the National League. During its single season of play, the league, which had a team in Cleveland, attracted greater attendance than the National League. Several Spiders players, including manager Pat Tebeau, joined the rival Cleveland team for the 1890 season. The enterprise collapsed when the league's backers withdrew support at the end of the season because of alleged financial losses.

One of these backers was Albert Johnson, Cleveland traction railway magnate and brother of future Cleveland mayor Tom L. Johnson, who also owned stock in the Brotherhood enterprise. The Johnson brothers, in their backing of the Players' League team, both showed their support of what was essentially a movement by organized labor and struck a blow against a traction business rival, Frank Robison.

OLIVER WENDELL "PATSY" TEBEAU (5 Dec. 1864–15 May 1918) came to the Cleveland Spiders professional baseball team in 1889 as a player and assumed the role of player-manager from 1890 to 1898. Tebeau's best years as a player were from 1893 to 1895, when he batted over .300. As a manager he was combative, often harassing opposing teams and umpires. His style kept the team in contention most of the time from 1892 to 1896. At the end of the 1898 season, the Spiders' owner, Frank Robison, angered by poor attendance, transferred Tebeau and the other talented players to the St. Louis team he had just purchased.

One of Robison's stockholders was businessman and political power broker Marcus A. Hanna, a man whom Tom Johnson would challenge in both the business and the political arenas in coming years.

Whatever the social and political ramifications involved in their establishment, the Spiders finally gave Cleveland a winner. Under the management of Pat Tebeau, who returned to the team after his brief sojourn in the Players' League, and with stellar players such as Cy Young, George Cuppy, John Clarkson, and catcher Charles Zimmer, the Spiders became contenders in the 1890s. Playing their home games at a new field, eventually to be known as League Park (the Payne Avenue stands had been hit by lightning and burned to the ground), on a Robison streetcar line at East 66th Street and Lexington Avenue, the team finished in second place in 1892 (it was also one of only two National League teams showing a profit that year). Third- and sixth-place finishes in 1893 and 1894, respectively, were followed by two second-place finishes in 1895 and 1896, which, in the pre–World Series era, qualified the Spiders for the Temple Cup playoffs with the league leader. In both instances the first-place team was the Orioles of Baltimore.

These two Temple Cup contests provide some insight into the nature of baseball and baseball crowds, which, despite the best efforts of the National League, continued often to consist of rowdy "fanatics" (fans). During the first best-of-seven series, the Spiders won the cup, assisted by local fans who bombarded the visiting Orioles with potatoes and other missiles. The series was clinched in Baltimore, where fan reaction was such that it "threatened [the Spiders'] safety." Perhaps the fan reaction was partly in response to the Cleveland club's style. Manager Tebeau was "an advocate of rowdy baseball." He once claimed that "a milk and water, goody-goody player can't ever wear a Cleveland uniform." In 1896 Baltimore gained its revenge and won the cup back with a four-game sweep.

The loss of the cup in 1896 signaled the beginning of the end for the Spiders, as they slipped to fifth place during the following two years. Attendance at home games dwindled. The loss of receipts and local loyalty angered Robison. He retaliated in 1898 by arbitrarily moving the best players from the Spiders to the St. Louis team he had just purchased. This made a poor team even worse. By 1899 the situation was so bad that only five hundred people attended the opening-day doubleheader. To remedy this, Robison decided not to play home games after July 1 but to move the team's home contests to other nearby cities. An attendance rise in Cleveland prior to the July 1 deadline did cause Robison to schedule some games in

OLD JUDGE CIGARETTES Goodwin & Co., New York.

1888 advertisement featuring Cleveland baseball star and future Hall of Famer Pat Tebeau. *National Baseball Library, Cooperstown, New York.*

Cleveland, but at any rate, the Spiders, who were now being called "The Misfits" and "The Wanderers," did not stand as a source of local pride. Winning two games in a row only once, the team finished the 1899 season with a 20 and 134 record. In 1900, when the National League decided to trim its roster to eight teams, Cleveland was one of the four cities dropped. Once again, Cleveland was without a profes-

Detailed drawing of League Park in 1924. *Cleveland Public Library.*

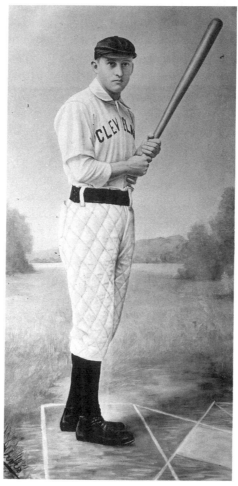

(LEFT) **Denton True "Cy" Young in uniform for the Cleveland American League team in 1910.** *Cleveland Press Collection, Cleveland State University.*

Jesse Cail "Crab" Burkett, ca. 1890s. *National Baseball Library, Cooperstown, New York.*

DENTON TRUE "CY" YOUNG (29 Mar. 1867–4 Nov. 1955), whose name personifies excellence in baseball pitching, played for the Cleveland Spiders of the National League from 1890 to 1898 and for the Cleveland team of the American League from 1909 to 1911. Born in Gilmore, Ohio, he compiled 511 career victories (289 NL and 222 AL), won 20 or more games 16 times, threw 3 no-hitters, and averaged 8 innings per game over his career. In 1956 the annual Cy Young Award was established to honor the outstanding pitchers in both leagues.

sional baseball team, but there were other sporting activities that would fill some of the void.

The prominence of baseball in the late nineteenth century somewhat obscures the fact that other recreational activities were taking place. These sports arose in some instances in reaction to the popular workingman's national pastime, and in others to provide participatory activity and entertainment for a population grown too large and too diverse to settle for a single sport.

The view of baseball as a "common" sport made it appear largely unsuitable to Cleveland's growing upper class as either a pastime or an investment by the late 1800s. Many may have shared an anglophilic view expressed in the *New York Times* on August 30, 1881, that compared cricket with baseball. The editorial noted that Americans had bypassed cricket some twenty-five years previously because they were unworthy of the game, preferring instead to play baseball, "an easy game that everybody can learn." The intimation was clear: baseball had no cachet. Wealthy Clevelanders, however, did not take up cricket, but rather concentrated on and expanded their antebellum interest in horseracing and other equine-based sports.

The interest in racing was most spectacularly visible during the winter months along Euclid Avenue, which by the 1870s had a reputation as one of the wealthiest and most beautiful residential streets in the nation. The snow-covered street was the site of numerous match races in which residents tested their horses and sleighs

HENRY KELSEY "HARRY K." DEVEREUX (10 Oct. 1859–1 May 1932), whose legendary contributions to harness racing earned him the title of "greatest driver of them all," was instrumental in establishing the sport in northeast Ohio. Devereux's racing feats included winning over 3,000 cups and ribbons during his life, as well as setting 14 racing and driving records. Devereux created the Gentlemen's Driving Club of Cleveland in 1895, organized the League of American Driving Clubs in 1901, and in 1908 financed the construction of Randall Park racetrack, which remained open until the 1970s.

JESSE CAIL "CRAB" BURKETT (12 Feb. 1870–27 May 1953) was an outfielder for the Cleveland Spiders of the National League from 1891 to 1898. Burkett shares the record with Ty Cobb and Roger Hornsby for hitting .400 or higher three times. His batting marks of .423 in 1895 and .410 in 1896 helped the Spiders gain a berth in the Temple Cup series each year. Transferred to St. Louis in 1899 by Spiders owner Frank D. Robison, Burkett finished his career in 1905 with a lifetime batting average of .342, and in 1946 was elected to the Baseball Hall of Fame.

against one another. By the 1880s and 1890s, when the event had become almost formalized, as many as thirty to forty sleighs awaited match races that ran from Case (East 40th) Street to Erie (East 9th) Street. Thousands lined the route. The drivers came from the city's first families: Perkins, Rockefeller, Gordon, Hanna, Corning, Garretson, and Devereux. Only with the advent of the automobile at the turn of the century did the races come to an end.

During the summer season these families patronized, both as participants and as spectators, the harness races held at the Glenville Race Track. Located on St. Clair between East 88th and East 101st streets, the track had been constructed in 1870 by the Cleveland Driving Park Company as part of the Northern Ohio Fair, which was sited across St. Clair. Although the fairgrounds were given up in 1881, the racetrack endured for almost another thirty years. The founders of the Driving Park Company included Frank Rockefeller, Sylvester Everett, Warren H. Corning, and How-

Harry K. Devereux finishes a trotting heat in 1906. *Western Reserve Historical Society.*

Harness racing at Glenville Track ca. 1900. *Western Reserve Historical Society.*

ard M. Hanna, names which exemplified the wealthy clientele attracted to the venture.

During the latter part of the nineteenth century, the track and its wealthy backers made Cleveland one of the major sites for harness racing. In 1872 the city joined with Buffalo, Utica, and Rochester to form the Quadrilateral Circuit, and within a year the four cities became part of the Grand Circuit, the major league of harness racing. Meets featuring locally bred horses and nationally noted trotters such as William H. Vanderbilt's Maud S. attracted the cream of Cleveland's society.

To further enhance the attraction of the races, Harry K. Devereux, Billy Edwards, and Daniel Rhodes Hanna organized the Gentlemen's Driving Club in 1895. This body promoted harness racing, eventually introduced trotters to the track (which had featured pacers), and began a series of afternoon matinee races which at times attracted more than 10,000 people. Of these three men, Devereux was the most noted amateur harness racer. The son of General John J. Devereux, one of the leading railroad managers in the Midwest, "Harry K." had a privileged upbringing (during which he served as the model for the drummer boy in Archibald Willard's painting *The Spirit of '76*). As a youth he became fascinated with horses and harness racing. Following his graduation from Yale, he began to invest his pocket money in the horses which he drove at the Glenville track. He became an accomplished driver, winning over 3,000 cups and ribbons during his amateur career and setting 14 driving and riding records.

Across St. Clair from the track was the Roadside Club, the site of postmatinee race dinners and celebrations, as well as the area's most noted casino. The track's appeal was not based totally on appreciation of fine horseflesh. Betting on the races and gambling at the club afterward were major attractions for Cleveland's social set. The scene at the Glenville track, as recorded by area photographers at the turn of the century, seemed to rival that at the Derby in England. Elegantly attired ladies and gentlemen watched the races from their carriages. Some of the carriages may have belonged to members of the Four-in-Hand Tandem Club, a local organization of bluebloods who emulated the English sport of coaching. Entourages of members,

in fine carriages pulled by matched teams and announced by coach horns, often visited the track as part of the annual social schedule.

By the early twentieth century, the track's one-mile oval had also become the site of major automotive races. Appropriately, Cleveland's auto industry, then the largest in the nation, often provided the Wintons, Baker electrics, and other machines tested at the track by daredevil drivers such as Barney Oldfield. The very industries that had made possible the spectators' wealth and the breeding of fine animals were producing a mechanical competitor that would cause upper-class interest in harness racing to wane. Nationally, the change was epitomized by the

Spectators in carriages view the action at Glenville track, ca. 1905. Western Reserve Historical Society.

The Four-in-Hand Tandem Club out on the road in 1903. Western Reserve Historical Society.

Barney Oldfield at Glenville Track in 1905. At the time, Cleveland's auto industry was the largest in the nation, and many of the cars were test-driven by "daredevils" such as Oldfield. *Western Reserve Historical Society.*

Vanderbilt family. Where once Maud S., William H. Vanderbilt's trotter, had been the talk of the town, now William K. Vanderbilt's "Vanderbilt Cup" auto races attracted the attention of the nation's upper classes. By World War I, harness races were largely passé in Cleveland.

Before that interest died, however, the Glenville track fell victim to reform when Frederick H. Goff, mayor of Glenville, banned betting at the facility in 1908. Goff, who that year became president of the Cleveland Trust Company and who would later go on to found the Cleveland Foundation, apparently was trying to make the city (legally annexed to Cleveland in 1905) conform to the moral expectations of the general community. Devereux and other racing promoters quickly overcame the blow. They incorporated their own village, North Randall, in 1908 to provide a new venue for trotting and betting. The new North Randall track would continue to run Grand Circuit trotting races until 1938, although interest in the sport waned rapidly after the 1910s. For many years, the chief industry of this new Cleveland community would be the breeding and training of race horses.

The cult of the horse as a basis for upper-class sports in Cleveland carried beyond the harness track. Whereas harness racing, particularly by trotters, was a largely American phenomenon, polo and riding to hounds had very British overtones. Their adoption by Cleveland's wealthier residents therefore had as much to do with making a proper social statement in the anglophilic world of American society as with enjoyment of the event itself. As early as 1897–99, a foxhunting group, the Cleveland Hunt, had been active. In 1908, however, the establishment of the Chagrin Valley Hunt Club provided a more permanent sponsor for the event. Established through the initiative of industrialist and sportsman Charles A. Otis, the group, originally called the Cuyahoga County Cross Country Riding Association, purchased English hounds from Canada and set up headquarters at the Maple Leaf Inn in Gates Mills. By the following year the group had purchased the inn and officially incorporated as the Chagrin Valley Hunt Club Company. Its membership, limited initially to 100 and then 150, rode to hounds through the Chagrin Valley, which by the time of World War I was becoming the site of the country estates of the city's business and industrial leadership.

The estates, kennels, stables, and open land to the east of Cleveland in Gates Mills, Hunting Valley, Kirtland, Waite Hill, and Wickliffe provided a location not only for foxhunts but also for another equine-based sport, polo. Although the sport would not prosper in the area until the 1920s, its origins date to 1911, when Clevelanders Edmund S. Burke, Jr., and Corliss E. Sullivan learned the game while wintering in South Carolina. Burke created a polo field at his Wickliffe estate and hired Earle Hopping to teach the game and coach. Burke even bought ponies for would-be polo players. By 1916, the Chagrin Valley Hunt Club had formed its own team and laid out a regulation field. Other fields were eventually laid out at the Kirtland Country Club and at the country farms of Walter C. White, John Sherwin, Jr., and Windsor T. White. However, it would not be until after World War I, the conflict that shook the empire with which the game was associated, that major organized intercity play would begin in the area.

If the more prosperous elements of Cleveland's population sought symbols of exclusivity in the sports they pursued, they certainly succeeded with those based on the ownership of horses and land. Polo and riding to hounds were available to only the very wealthy. Other sports arose in post–Civil War Cleveland that provided both enjoyment and status for those citizens who were not quite country squires but certainly were not day laborers. A host of athletic activities, beginning with indoor ice skating in the 1860s, continuing with roller skating in the 1880s, and climaxing most visibly with the bicycle craze of the 1880s and 1890s, appealed to a growing middle class with leisure time and the funds to purchase the necessary equipment.

Bicycling, when first introduced locally in the late 1870s, was an expensive, somewhat hazardous pastime, as the equipment consisted of the fifty-eight-inch

Bicycle messengers take a break for lunch, ca. 1900. Bicycles served both practical and recreational needs well into the 20th century. *Cleveland Press Collection, Cleveland State University.*

high-wheel "ordinary," which cost $150 (when the average yearly income of an industrial worker might be $400). One of the first citizens to own and operate a high-wheel ordinary was Jeptha Homer Wade, Jr., a member of one of the city's wealthiest families. By the mid-1880s, the modern bicycle (with two wheels of equal size and a chain drive) had been introduced, and the vehicle became more accessible in terms of operation and cost. The mid-1890s, when an estimated 50,000 two- and three-wheelers were operated in the city, marked the high point of the bicycle craze in Cleveland. Perhaps one of every six of the estimated 300,000 Clevelanders owned a bicycle. The production of bicycles by local concerns such as the White Sewing Machine Company and that owned by Alexander Winton became an important facet of the local economy—one which would in many instances lead later to the production of automobiles. While many Clevelanders used their bicycles for practical transportation to and from the office, they and others also used them for excursions and races such as those sponsored by local chapters of the League of American Wheelmen, the first local chapter of which, the Cleveland Bicycle Club, had formed in 1879. They, along with other Clevelanders, also watched bicycle races. These included indoor events, such as a six-day women's race held at the Central Armory in 1896.

The participation of women in cycling both for recreation and in competitive events in the nineteenth century was echoed in two other sports, each with a degree of social cachet, that developed in Cleveland after the Civil War. The games of tennis and golf were more exclusive than bicycling but more accessible than equine-centered sports. Although the true origins of tennis derived from the twelfth- and thirteenth-century French game of *jeu de paume*, the game that arrived in Cleveland was based on the outdoor racket and ball game Sphairistike invented by Major Walter Wingfield in England in 1873. Within seven years of the publication of Wingfield's rules, tennis had made its way to Cleveland. Not unexpectedly, the new British rage of lawn tennis was first played at a Euclid Avenue residence, that of Frank Billings, in 1880. The informal game at the East 88th and Euclid location soon moved to the front lawn of the George Worthington house, also on Euclid Avenue, but a bit closer to the city.

The game was formalized in Cleveland in the 1880s with the creation of the Buckeye and East End tennis clubs, both of which played in the Euclid-Willson (East 55th Street) Avenue area. In 1890 the East End Club, under the leadership of industrialist and businessman George Worthington, sponsored the first city tournament. The club prospered as other members of Cleveland society took up the game. It eventually established headquarters at Euclid and Kennard (East 46th) Street, and when court demands became greater, it built new ones on Carnegie west of East 77th Street. In 1914, the new courts were the site of the Ohio State Open. The cross-gender acceptability of tennis (it was considered a genteel activity suitable for women) led to a series of city women's championships sponsored by the East End Club. Elizabeth Dean Sprague won the local championship for three consecutive years, 1899–1901. A second Cleveland woman, Mary K. Brown, went on to win the United States women's championship in three straight years, 1912–14. In the 1920s, Brown would team up with nationally renowned Helen Wills to win the women's doubles championship. The outstanding male player of the period, T. Sterling Beckwith, Jr., won both local and state championships. His family home, on Euclid Avenue near East 40th, was one of the few residences of Millionaires' Row to survive into the 1990s, at which time it was home to the University Club and, appropriately enough, to the tennis courts of that club.

By the beginning of World War I, local lawn tennis was complemented and nearly supplanted by tennis played clay courts maintained by some of the area's

"Old-fashioned tennis": Edith Farrassey of West High returns a serve in a match, 2 August 1912. *Cleveland Press Collection, Cleveland State University.*

private clubs, including ones at Edgewater, Nela Park, and the Cleveland Yacht Club. It is estimated that 90 percent of the area's players belonged to such clubs. At that time the game was still accessible only to those with the funds for equipment and club membership. Within those restrictions, however, it was one of the few

T. STERLING BECKWITH, JR. (5 Feb. 1865–17 Feb. 1943) was a wealthy Cleveland sportsman and fine amateur golf and tennis player, winning the city amateur golf championship in 1900 and 1901 and the first Ohio amateur golf championship in 1904. Beckwith also won city and state tennis championships in the 1890s.

sports in which women could take a recognized leadership role by the turn of the century.

Women also participated in golf, another British import that arrived to satisfy the leisure needs of Cleveland's leading citizens in the 1890s. Although golf was probably played in the American colonies, it was not until the 1880s that organized golf clubs began to appear in the eastern parts of the United States. The large amount of land required for a course and the extended time necessary for playing the game made the sport initially accessible only to the wealthy. That requirement, as well as its ancient Scottish origins, provided it with great social attractiveness.

Cleveland industrialist and philanthropist Samuel Mather introduced the game to the city. While out east on business in 1895, Mather had played a round of golf at the St. Andrews course in Mount Hope, New York, one of the first and most prestigious clubs in the nation. He took a liking to the game and upon his return to

T. Sterling Beckwith out on the links at Shaker Country Club, 1932. *Cleveland Press Collection, Cleveland State University.*

Cleveland organized the Cleveland Golf Club, the membership of which, he hoped, would include many of the social and business leaders of the city. The club opened its nine-hole course in Glenville (now Bratenahl) on July 13, 1895, with an exhibition match between T. Sterling Beckwith, Jr., one of the area's foremost tennis players, and J. D. Maclennin. By 1897 Clevelanders had become skilled enough in the game to defeat a team of Buffalo, New York, golfers. The golf club was sited next to the Country Club, in which Mather was also an officer. Loosely affiliated at first, the two organizations eventually merged under the Country Club's name in

Bill Burke and Sam Snead are surrounded by the gallery at Oakwood Country Club, August 1938. *Cleveland Press Collection, Cleveland State University.*

THE OAKWOOD CLUB (est. 1905), located at 1516 Warrensville Center in University Heights, was Cleveland Heights' first major Jewish country club. Initially founded as a golfing club for the area's Jewish sportsmen, Oakwood was later expanded to provide social and recreational activities. The 18-hole golf course was host to the 1921 Western Open. In 1931 Oakwood merged with the Excelsior Club, an exclusive Jewish social club. That year also saw the organization of the Oakwood Women's Golf Association. During World War II, Oakwood's clubhouse was used as a barracks by the U.S. Army.

COBURN HASKELL (1868–14 Dec. 1922), prominent Cleveland businessman and sportsman, is recognized as the inventor of the modern golf ball. While working for the M. A. Hanna Co., Haskell—an avid golfer—patented a ball with a rubber-bound core on 11 April 1899. In 1901 he created the Haskell Golf Ball Co., producer of the "Haskell Golf Ball," which soon replaced the gutta-percha ball and revolutionized golf ball manufacturing. Designed for greater distance, the Haskell ball helped to reduce scores. In 1917, Haskell sold the design patents and dissolved the Haskell Golf Ball Company.

1902. By that time Cleveland's first resident professional, Joseph Mitchell of Scotland, was on hand to advise the players.

The appeal of golf was initially quite limited, even within the social class with which it was associated. A thirty-six-hole exhibition at the Cleveland Golf Club by Harry Vardon, then the greatest British golfer, attracted only fifty people to the course in 1900. Interest did grow, however, and by 1915 seven clubs were located in Cuyahoga County. The first club established after Mather's pioneer venture was the Euclid Club, founded in 1900 in Cleveland Heights (in the area bounded roughly by Fairmount, North Park, Cedar, and Coventry). The Mayfield Country Club, which opened in 1910, drew so heavily on membership of the Euclid Club that the two merged, and the Euclid property was developed as a prime residential area. The

Coburn Haskell's contribution to golf—the invention of the modern golf ball, capable of mass production, as seen here at a golf ball factory in 1932. *Cleveland Press Collection, Cleveland State University.*

Dover Bay Country Club was also active by early in the century, with some authorities claiming that golf may have been played at that Bay Village site before Samuel Mather introduced the game in Bratenahl. The origins of the Oakwood Club, which opened its nine-hole course in 1906 on a site near Mayfield and Noble roads, demonstrated the exclusivity of golf and the divisions within Cleveland society. Oakwood's founders were members of the city's Jewish community. The fortunes of these wealthy merchants and businessmen were of no consequence, as their religion effectively barred any chance of membership in either the Country Club or the Euclid Club. Their only recourse was to establish their own facility.

One Clevelander had a club to himself. John D. Rockefeller was perhaps the only person in the city with sufficient resources to construct his own nine-hole course. He built it on his Forest Hill estate in East Cleveland, using it both to entertain guests and for his own pleasure. An avid golfer, Rockefeller pursued the game into the 1930s, when he was in his nineties, although by then he had long since given up his Forest Hill residence.

The rapidity with which golf engaged the interest of wealthy Clevelanders after 1900 was due in part to the example set by Rockefeller and the advocacy of men such as Samuel Mather. It was due also to a change in the game made possible by a Cleveland inventor, Coburn Haskell. Married to the daughter of the wealthy Howard M. Hanna, Haskell worked for the M. A. Hanna Company and pursued golf as a recreation. Dissatisfied with the then current gutta-percha golf ball, which gave little distance for the effort, Haskell, in conjunction with Bertram G. Work of the B. F. Goodrich Company, invented the modern rubber-core ball, which he patented in April 1899. The invention allowed Haskell to retire from the family business and made the game more pleasurable for golfers throughout the world.

The city's position in the sport and the growth in local interest were attested by the tournaments that began to be held at the different clubs. The first was the Western Open, a national amateur event, which was held at the Euclid Club in 1902. The tournament returned to Cleveland in 1915 and was played at the Mayfield Club. The Euclid Club hosted the Ohio State Golf Tournament in 1910. By 1906, district amateur tournaments were being held in Cleveland, and in 1917 the Cleveland District Golf Association was formed to oversee the growing local sport, which would include interclub matches by the following year.

The entry of women into the sport was exceedingly rapid. An informal women's city championship had taken place as early as 1897 at the Country Club, with Mrs. Kenyon V. Painter as the first champion. Local women's championships began on a regular basis in 1909. One of the most able players was Ruth Chisholm, a member of a family that owned one of the city's major iron and steel companies. She won the women's title in 1910 and 1912–13. Despite club membership discrimi-

Female golf star Ruth Chisholm at a social gathering in 1909. *Cleveland Public Library.*

Native American lacrosse team in the 1870s. Lacrosse was one of many popular athletic events held in Cleveland during the period. *Western Reserve Historical Society.*

nation, the competition was open to all golfers. Mrs. Alexander Printz, wife of a prominent Jewish clothing manufacturer, won the title in 1919. By 1923, women's involvement in local golf led to the founding of the Cleveland Women's Golf Association.

The twin developments of organized sport for economic gain (principally baseball) and exclusive pastimes for limited segments of the population loom large in the history of sports in Cleveland during the period from 1860 to 1920. The fact that baseball evolved into perhaps the major American sport of the twentieth century is partial reason for its strong historical recognition, while the families and wealth associated with equine sports, tennis, and golf have tended to make information about these activities more historically accessible. The fact that these formerly exclusive pastimes found a broader base in the next century also raised interest about their histories.

Less recognized in the city's nineteenth-century history are other, less spectacular activities that sometimes involved broader segments of the population. Chief among these, perhaps, is what was once called pedestrianism, which evolved into modern track and field. Walking, sprinting, and distance-running competitions have deep historical roots. County fairs in England had, and still have, running and racing events. Professional running and walking contests were recorded in sixteenth-century England. British immigrants brought this tradition with them to America, where the pedestrian events eventually were joined by a variety of other activities, including jumping, weight throwing, and weight lifting, which by the end of the Civil War were categorized as "athletics." Until the 1880s in cities such as Cleveland, these events took place either informally at picnics and fairs, or as professional contests with paid admission and cash prizes for the victors. In contrast to baseball, track events in the United States moved away from professionalism to become a predominantly amateur sport by the end of the century.

Cleveland's first major involvement with pedestrianism seems to have been sparked by its reception of noted long-distance walker Edward Payson Weston in 1867. On his way from Portland, Maine, to Chicago, Weston passed through Cleveland, spurring the development of a number of walking clubs. How many Clevelanders later tried to achieve one of the grueling goals of the pedestrian, walking one hundred miles in twenty-four hours, is unknown. The following year Weston, who had become so idolized that he set styles for clothing, hats, and gloves, appeared again in Cleveland. This time he put on a bravura indoor performance at Case Hall, where he walked twenty-five miles in five hours and then walked one mile backward in twenty minutes. He went on from his paid performance to lecture on "Athletic Sports" at the city's Industrial School.

While Clevelanders paid to watch Weston walk, they also put up money to watch other athletic events in the 1860s, including a relay race pitting three Native Americans against horses at the Cleveland Driving Park in 1867. To what degree local citizens patronized more conventional races and events in the years 1860–1880 is hard to determine. It can, however, be surmised that races and other "athletic" contests took place at the picnics and celebrations that were held by Clevelanders. Many of these were sponsored by the ethnic societies found among the English, Irish, Scots, and Germans who were predominant in the population by the 1870s, as well as by the labor unions that became a part of local life in the 1870s and 1880s.

By the 1880s, more formal local track-and-field activity had moved toward the arena of amateurism, with sponsorship coming from three general areas: local colleges, the YMCA, and athletic clubs. In 1885, for instance, the Cleveland Athletic Club (an organization headed by Cleveland baseball owner Frank DeHaas Robison) sponsored its first summer meet. It featured foot races and bicycle races involving athletes from throughout the Midwest. Although the 100-yard dash was won (in 9.8 seconds) by a professional, H. M. Johnson, he received only $20 as his prize. This gentlemen's club seems during its history to have had the dual purpose of promoting amateur athletics and entertaining its members. In addition to the annual meet, the club's members (over 500 by 1892) watched boxing and wrestling matches featuring some of the best fighters of the period in the club gymnasium situated on Euclid Avenue near East 14th Street. By the 1890s the members had formed one of the finest amateur baseball teams in the area, and also provided sponsorship for local amateur athletes, including Charles W. "Billy" Stage, the one-time holder of the national amateur 100-yard-dash record.

Stage's amateur career was initially associated with Western Reserve University, where, as a member of the Adelbert class of 1892, he was one of the school's best all-around athletes. In addition to captaining the school's football team, he set school records for the 100-yard dash, the standing high jump, the standing broad jump, and the standing hop-step-and-jump. "Athletics" at local colleges came into their own during the 1880s and 1890s, spurred in part by an increased national emphasis on amateurism, a move evidenced in particular by the creation of the Amateur Athletic Union in 1888. In 1902 Western Reserve University joined with Case School of Applied Science, Ohio State University, Oberlin College, Ohio Wesleyan University, and Kenyon College in forming the Ohio Collegiate Athletic Association. The first joint track meet sponsored by the association took place at the Glenville Rack Track in that same year.

The amateurization of "athletics" unfortunately tended to narrow participation in track and field and make such activities more elite than they had been. When prize monies were available, any skilled runner, for instance, would have the oppor-

CHARLES W. "BILLY" STAGE (26 Nov. 1868–17 May 1946) was a versatile athlete at Adelbert College of Western Reserve University as a member of the track and baseball teams, and captain of the university football team in 1891. He also worked as a National Baseball League umpire while a student at Adelbert and Western Reserve Law School. At the 1893 Columbian Exposition in Chicago, Stage won the 100-yard dash in 9.8 seconds and the 220 in 21.8—both remarkable achievements at the time.

tunity to hone his ability, since the purse being offered constituted his wages. By the 1890s, purses were fewer and national attention was focused on runners sponsored by exclusive athletic clubs or by colleges. Such athletes were viewed as running for "pure sport." Of course, one needed either connections for club affiliation or money for college (in a prescholarship era) to be able to compete. The establishment of the modern Olympic games in 1896 signified the almost complete transfer of prestige to the amateur athlete.

Perhaps only one venue remained open to the aspiring athlete without funds or backing—that was the Young Men's Christian Association. Cleveland's YMCA had been established in 1854. After becoming inactive during the Civil War, it reemerged in 1867. The initial emphasis of the YMCA was on maintaining Christian values among the young men coming to the city. This it did largely by sponsoring lectures and providing supervised housing. In 1881, under the leadership of a new president, Joseph Merian, the Cleveland YMCA seemingly shifted direction by beginning education and physical culture programs. This new emphasis on physical culture, how-

1895 Western Reserve University yearbook photo of track and football star Charles W. Stage. *Case Western Reserve University Archives.*

ever, was also geared to the YMCA's primary Christian purpose. Under the then growing doctrine of "muscular Christianity," a sound body was viewed as critical to the complete moral and spiritual development of the individual. More directly, the gymnasium and other athletic activities offered by the YMCA served to keep young men out of the pool halls and permitted them a safe, athletic outlet for their carnal energies. Whatever the rationale behind its establishment, the athletic program at the YMCA—which eventually included set exercises, running, and other track events—provided relatively open training for would-be athletes in Cleveland.

Those Clevelanders who patronized the YMCA or attended the track meets

Young girls competing at a picnic foot race, illustrating the popularity of "pedestrian" sports during the era, ca. 1912. *Western Reserve Historical Society.*

The conclusion of a city track meet 100-yard dash, 18 May 1926. Track-and-field competition emerged as a cornerstone of city-wide scholastic athletic activities. *Cleveland Press Collection, Cleveland State University.*

Young boys straining to top the chin-up bar at the YMCA in July 1941. The YMCA endeavored to keep young men off the streets and provide safe and supervised athletic training. *Cleveland Press Collection, Cleveland State University.*

sponsored by local colleges or organizations such as the Cleveland Athletic Club represented only one facet of the city's post–Civil War population. Unlikely to be found at these events were the non-English foreign-born, who came to Cleveland in huge numbers in the years from 1860 to 1920. In 1860 over 44 percent of the city's population was of foreign birth, with most having come from Ireland and Ger-

Photo of a Cleveland German Turner group in 1910. The German community of Cleveland utilized Turnverein gymnastics to build sound minds and bodies, and to focus on nationalistic pride. *Western Reserve Historical Society.*

many. By 1900 over 40,000 Germans lived in the city, and by 1920, one-third of the nearly 800,000 people in Cleveland were of foreign birth. Their origins represented most of the ethnic groupings to be found on the European continent. Members of several of these communities brought to Cleveland a European system of athletics that, like that of the YMCA, worked to build a sound body, but focused on serving nationalistic rather than Christian purposes.

Within the large German community, this movement centered in the Turnverein, and within a number of the Slavic communities it centered in the Sokol hall. Both organizations focused athletic activities around gymnastics—using parallel bars, vaulting horses, the side horse, and horizontal bar—and massed coordinated exercises. Both worked to achieve better health and sound bodies for their members and, particularly, to imbue them with feelings of patriotism for their respective homelands. The German Turner movement had been established in 1811 by Friedrich Ludwig Jahn to help prepare German youth to combat the Napoleonic menace to Prussia. Later, after the 1848 revolutions, the movement would focus on the creation of a united Germany and was actually considered subversive by the leaders of some German states. The Slavic Sokols stemmed from the work of two Czechs, Miroslav Tyrs and Jindrich Fuegner, in 1862. Their goal was to build a sense of racial pride among the Czechs that would eventually lead to the independence of their nation from the Hapsburgs. Eventually other Slavic groups emulated the Czechs and established their own Sokols.

The first of these groups to be established in Cleveland was the German Socialer Turnverein, which was created in 1867. By the turn of the century it owned a substantial three-story hall on Lorain Avenue. Other Turner groups, including the Voerwarts Turnverein, served Germans in the East 55th Street area on the other side of town. In 1879 local Czechs established the Sokol Cech, reportedly the second such organization in the United States. By 1920, six Czech Sokols had been established, along with Sokols representing the Polish, Serbian, Slovenian, and Slovak communities of Cleveland. Their gymnastic halls could be found in the Broadway–East 55th and Clark Avenue Czech communities, near the Fleet Avenue Polish community, and along St. Clair Avenue, where the city's south Slavic groups (Slovenes, Croatians, and Serbs) had taken up residence. Unlike the gymnasiums owned or sponsored by athletic clubs or the YMCA, these facilities were used by both men and women, although in separate sessions. For first-generation immigrants they provided a sports venue of great significance within their respective communities and became a central aspect of neighborhood life.

The children of those neighborhoods, however, were another matter. As Cleveland grew to become an industrial metropolis with a diverse population, it came to have a veritable warren of neighborhoods, each ethnically or socially different from the next. In some, housing and living conditions were abominable. Native Clevelanders looked upon the continuing fragmentation of their city and wondered whether the inhabitants of these communities, who spoke different languages and followed different customs, could ever become part of American society. In particular, the fate of the children, who could be found playing on the streets throughout the city, was a matter of concern. How could they be saved from lives of proverty and crime? How could they be molded into good Americans?

A partial answer to the question was provided through organized sports and play, brought into the city's immigrant neighborhood through the settlement house movement. Begun in England and transplanted to the United States by the 1880s, the settlement house movement rested on a very basic premise: Educated individuals, usually of middle-class background, took up residence in the midst of urban neighborhoods and there used their knowledge and good will to help area residents

A young female gymnast of a Czech Sokol group performs on the uneven bars at a holiday exhibition, ca. 1912. The gymnastic events promoted by the Sokol groups were vital organizational tools for many Slavic ethnic communities. *Western Reserve Historical Society.*

The Alta House, which began settlement work in 1900, and the Hiram House, founded in 1896, were two of Cleveland's foremost settlement houses in the early 1900s and were instrumental in bringing organized sports and play to their respective immigrant communities. These agencies sponsored clubs and provided playgrounds and gymnasiums for local youths. Basketball in particular was a popular sport because of its ideal elements—minimal equipment was required, and it taught sportsmanship and teamwork. Ethnic rivalries, however, added an extra tinge of excitement to many competitions.

The Hiram House boys' basketball team, ca. 1910. Basketball suited the athletic needs of settlement houses because it was contained, it was competitive, it taught teamwork, and, most important, it was an American game. *Western Reserve Historical Society.*

The CLEVELAND BLUES was the American League baseball team which eventually became the Cleveland Indians. Ben Johnson, founder of the American League, moved the minor-league Cedar Rapids team to Cleveland in 1900, and the "Bluebirds" finished in 7th place in 1901 as a major-league team, last in nearly all team categories, and lowest in attendance. The following year Napoleon Lajoie came to the Blues, and by 1905 the team was known as the "Naps."

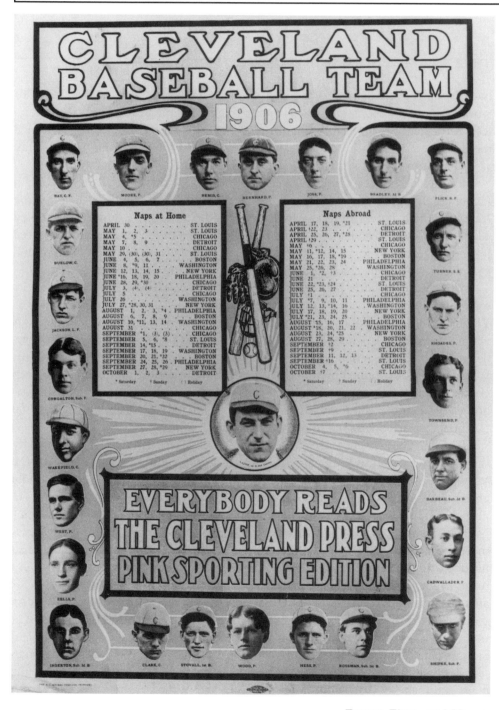

This Cleveland "Naps" roster issued by the *Cleveland Press* in 1906 shows the wide influence which Napoleon Lajoie (*center*) had upon his ballclub and his fans. *Cleveland Press Collection, Cleveland State University.*

ADRIAN "ADDIE" JOSS (12 Apr. 1880–14 Apr. 1911) pitched for the Cleveland team in the American League from 1902 to 1910. His career earned-run average of 1.88 per 9-inning game was the second-lowest in major-league history. He completed a remarkable 90 percent of all games he started in his career, and compiled a 160–97 won-loss record. Although a minimum of 10 seasons is required for a player to be considered for entrance into the Baseball Hall of Fame, the Committee on Veterans waived the rule for Joss in 1978, and the pitcher was voted into the Cooperstown, N.Y., shrine.

by providing classes for children and adults, establishing day-care facilities for working mothers, sponsoring clubs, and arranging for the provision of social services. Settlements that began with the residency of three or four college-educated men and women in a rented house might evolve into a major neighborhood facility with dozens of workers, meeting rooms, a playground, and a gymnasium.

By the early 1900s Cleveland had a number of settlements, including Hiram House on Orange Avenue at East 27th Street, Alta House on Mayfield Road in Little Italy, Goodrich House on St. Clair Avenue, and the Jewish Council Educational Alliance on lower Woodland Avenue. For the children in the neighborhoods served by these agencies, the settlements' chief attractions were their playgrounds and gymnasiums. And the chief attraction in the gymnasium was basketball.

Unlike other sports played by Americans, basketball had not evolved on its own, but had been invented to fill a specific need. In creating the game for the YMCA in 1891, James Naismith designed an indoor activity that was not violent (it was not to involve any body contact or the driving of a ball through a ground-level defended goal), that tested coordination, and that was physically demanding. This latter factor was specified by the YMCA, which needed more active games to keep youth attracted to its gymnasiums. It was also an ideal game for the settlement house—it required a minimum of equipment, it was American, and it had the potential to teach sportsmanship and teamwork.

The first games were played in Cleveland at the Central YMCA in 1894, and by the following year the YMCA had organized an intermural league. It was in the schools and, particularly, the settlement houses, however, that the game found its greatest success. By the early 1900s, Hiram House was hosting a number of games in its gymnasium, with teams made up from different segments of its neighborhood's population, or representing other settlements and area schools. By 1915, the settlement teams had become part of the Old Boys' Workers Group, a league that also included teams from the YMCA and from municipal playgrounds. High-school teams had separated into their own league, the Senate, in 1904. Naismith's hopes for an active but nonviolent sport were shattered by the reality of the game played in local settlement gyms. By 1900 the local YMCA was deploring the growing roughness of the game and advising against the formation of additional leagues. At Hiram House, games played between teams of differing ethnic backgrounds—most often Jewish versus Italian—were the cause of near-riots as the players battled on the court and their fans battled in the gymnasium and in the street afterward. In 1907,

Adrian "Addie" Joss, shown here ca. 1907, completed an amazing 90 percent of all the games he started; he pitched two perfect games in an eight-year career. *Western Reserve Historical Society.*

NAPOLEON "NAP" LAJOIE (5 Sept. 1875–7 Feb. 1959), also known as "Larry," was a baseball player with the American League Cleveland ballclub from 1902 to 1914. An exceptional hitter and fielder, Lajoie was the player-manager of the team from 1905 to 1909; the team was called the "Naps" in his honor. The sixth man to be voted into the Hall of Fame in 1937, Lajoie had a career batting average of .339, with 3,251 hits during his 21-year major-league career.

in one instance at Hiram House, a group of knife-wielding Italians chased the Jewish basketball team out of the gym after a game. Fifty years after inventing the game, in his 1941 memoirs, Naismith would strongly criticize officials who had permitted the sport to become so physical. What Naismith had not foreseen was that basketball would become part of urban culture, a rough-and-tumble world where youths of various races and nationalities tested themselves against their peers and sought to prove their prowess in surroundings far less genteel than the YMCA gymnasiums.

There was, however, one other sport that gained the loyalty of the youth of Cleveland's urban neighborhoods in the early 1900s, one which by that time had begun to transcend the boundaries of race, class, and nationality. Among all of the growing number of athletic activities in the twentieth-century city, only baseball was viewed as broadly representative of the community's athletic "standing," and only baseball provided heroes with an almost universal community appeal. Although baseball was widely played on city streets and by amateur clubs sponsored, eventually, by athletic clubs, businesses, churches, schools, colleges, and settlement houses, Clevelanders looked to their professional team as a symbol of their city.

Following the embarrassing episodes preceding the demise of the Spiders in 1900, it is a wonder that local citizens would have had any desire to see professional baseball return to Cleveland. But in a pattern that would be repeated countless times in the decades to come, Clevelanders brushed aside embarrassment and team mismanagement and continued to support the professional game. In 1901 they had a new team to cheer for. The Cleveland Blues (the franchise ancestor of the Indians) were a charter member of the new American League (in 1991, the Cleveland team, along with those of Boston, Detroit, and Chicago, would be one of only four charter members still playing in their original city). The new league, established to challenge the National League, survived the so-called baseball war of 1901–1903, in which the new franchises attempted to lure players away from the older circuit. It emerged as a full-fledged partner when a new "National Agreement" was signed in 1903. This set up the mechanism for the World Series playoff, and also guaranteed that both leagues would honor reserve clauses.

The owners of the Cleveland franchise, coal merchant Charles W. Somers, his father, and clothing store owner John F. Kilfoyle, did not, as in the case of past challenges to the National League, view their effort as one directed to give the players latitude in decision making or to reform the game; they saw it as a pure and simple business proposition. Somers knew that the Cleveland franchise's health depended on the success of the new league, so he not only invested heavily in his

Cleveland Naps player/manager Napoleon Lajoie jumps for a catch, ca. 1905. *Cleveland Press Collection, Cleveland State University.*

ELMER H. FLICK (11 Jan. 1876–9 Jan. 1971) began his baseball career as an outfielder with Philadelphia in 1898. Moving to Cleveland in 1902, he played there for 9 seasons, winning the American League batting title in 1905. Considered one of the top hitters at the turn of the century, Flick compiled a lifetime batting average of .315 during his 13-year major-league career and was voted into baseball's Hall of Fame in 1963.

Nap Lajoie hands a baseball to a young fan, Petey Powers, ca. 1911. Lajoie was perhaps Cleveland's first widely recognized sports hero during the early 1900s. *Western Reserve Historical Society.*

Elmer Flick prepares to catch a flyball, ca. 1916. *Western Reserve Historical Society.*

own team but also spent nearly $1 million bankrolling other teams and players in the American League.

The success of the franchise was ensured, however, when second baseman Napoleon Lajoie was acquired from the Philadelphia Athletics in June 1902. In 1901, Lajoie had achieved the astounding batting average of .422, so his arrival in Cleveland was an event of great significance. One of his early appearances attracted the largest weekday crowd in the history of local professional baseball. Named player-manager of the team in 1905, Lajoie led the club to a second-place finish in 1908. He was perhaps the first widely recognized sports hero in Cleveland. His stature was such that the team, which had been renamed the Broncos, was renamed the Naps in his honor in 1903. The drawing power of Lajoie and the growing interest in baseball were such that League Park, Frank Robison's trolley-car stadium and the home of the new American League team, had to be expanded. Originally built to accommodate 9,000 fans, the park was expanded to a capacity of 27,000 in 1909.

LOUIS FRANCIS "CHIEF" SOCKALEXIS (24 Oct. 1871–24 Dec. 1913) was a Penobscot Indian who played outfield for the Cleveland Spiders from 1897 to 1899. He joined the Spiders in 1897, hitting home runs in his first two at-bats and finishing the season with a .338 average. Tragically, Sockalexis's alcoholism ruined his exceptional athletic talents, and he was released by the Spiders in 1899. In 1915, the Cleveland American League team, in need of a nickname, held a contest and chose "Indians," submitted in honor of the Chief, Louis Sockalexis, making him the only individual after whom a major-league team is named.

The second-place finish of 1908, however, appeared to be a fluke, and Lajoie's playing prowess faded. In 1914 the team (renamed the Molly McGuires in 1912) finished with a dismal 51 and 102 record. Lajoie was traded the following year. Owner Somers, nearly $2 million in debt, was advised to sell the team. That year a syndicate led by James C. Dunn, a Chicago businessman, bought the franchise for $500,000. The transfer of the team to nonlocal ownership hinted at the fact that baseball was becoming a major business commodity. Perhaps the only local ties it retained were those of civic pride and fan loyalty.

The sale of the franchise signaled a completely new era for the team. It was renamed the Indians, partially in response to a newspaper poll of local fans, who remembered the days in the 1890s when the Cleveland Spiders were sometimes called the Indians in honor of one of their star players, Louis "Chief" Sockalexis, a Penobscot Indian. More important, the team acquired centerfielder Tristam "Tris" Speaker from the Boston Red Sox at a cost of $50,000. The American League's most valuable player in 1912, Speaker demanded, and got, $10,000 of the purchase price before he joined the Cleveland team in 1916. Playing for a $40,000 annual salary, the highest in baseball (the average Ohio worker earned $672 annually in 1920), Speaker won the league batting championship during his first year with the Indians. In 1919 he was named player-manager and led the team to a second-place finish. In the following year he would lead Cleveland to its first World Series title.

Perhaps the changes that had taken place in local baseball are best summarized in an early movie made in Cleveland. *Perils of Society* was a photoplay produced by the socially prominent families of Cleveland in 1916 to be shown as a benefit to raise funds for World War I Belgian orphans. Acted entirely by members of the city's leading families, the film provides an excellent review of the leisure activities of the local social set. In the movie a group of supposed English nobles are "shown the town." They watch or participate in yachting, tennis, golf, polo, and riding to hounds. And, they are taken to a baseball game at League Park, where they meet Tris Speaker. Baseball had come a long way from being a Sabbath-breaking, boozy entertainment for workingmen. Indeed, it had become America's game—the embodiment of all the virtues of the society that had invented it.

The sixty-year local evolution of baseball from a pick-up game once played on Public Square, to an acceptable, regulated, marketable commodity promising

Penobscot Indian Louis "The Chief" Sockalexis, the namesake of the modern-day Cleveland Indians. *National Baseball Library, Cooperstown, New York.*

Addie Joss All Star Game, ca. 1906. *Courtesy of Del Bethel.*

returns for investors and incentives for good workers, is perhaps the overriding symbol of sports development in Cleveland during the 1860–1920 period. Other sports had risen to serve the needs of the wealthy and the workers, and to meet purposes as diverse as indicating social status and teaching Christian values. None, however, fit the overall needs of a cosmopolitan, business-oriented city as well as baseball. In the next thirty years other sports would attempt to follow this example, and in doing so would provide Clevelanders with a multitude of diversions and heroes in an era of prosperity, depression, and war.

TRISTAM "TRIS" SPEAKER (4 Apr. 1888–8 Dec. 1958) played for the Cleveland Indians from 1916 to 1926, and was the player-manager of the Indians' first world championship team, in 1920. Acquired from Boston in 1916, Speaker hit .386 and won the league batting title in his first season in Cleveland. Named manager in 1919, he hit .388 and set a record of 11 consecutive hits in 1920 as Cleveland defeated Brooklyn in the World Series. Speaker batted .345 with 3,515 hits over his 22-year career, and was elected to the Baseball Hall of Fame in 1937.

Ted Easterly Herrie Wagner (Manager) Clyde Milan Walter Johnson • 1936 Gabby Street Bobby Wallace • 1953 Frank Baker (Home Run) • 1955 James McAleer (Mgr of All Stars) Sam Crawford • 1957 Tris Speaker • 1937 Hal Chase Russell Ford Joe Wood Paddy Livingston Herman Schaefer (Germany) Tyrus Cobb (Ty) • 1936 Eddie Collins 1939 Jack Graney of Cleveland (2nd time in photo)

Indians star and manager Tris Speaker is congratulated by Brooklyn Dodgers manager Wilbert Robinson after the Indians' victory in the 1920 World Series. *Western Reserve Historical Society.*

Everybody's Games Are Good Business in Cleveland, 1920–1945

In the 1920s and 1930s, *Cleveland Press* photographer Louis Van Oeyen may have been considered by many people, adults and children alike, to be the luckiest man in Cleveland. Van Oeyen, who had begun his photojournalistic career with snapshots of a tunnel disaster at Cleveland's water intake crib in 1901, had, by the 1910s, become the city's preeminent sports photographer. With a home located just blocks away from League Park, he spent hours there hobnobbing with the greats of the golden era of baseball. It was reported that Babe Ruth would join Van Oeyen at his home after a game for some Prohibition-era beer stored in the family icebox. His was truly a job to be envied in an era when men with names such as Ruth, Gehrig,

LOUIS A. VAN OEYEN (17 Jan. 1865–12 Dec. 1946) was the dean of local newspaper photographers from the early years in the century when he became a full-time member of the *Cleveland Press* staff until his retirement in 1937. In nearly 4 decades with the newspaper, his favorite assignments were those connected with baseball, and he was a familiar figure on the sidelines. Van Oeyen photographed most of the major sports events, catastrophes, and celebrities reported in Cleveland during his long career. His were among the first photographs with the fast new lenses which could ''stop'' action, instead of requiring poses.

Famed sports photographer Louis Van Oeyen grasps the *Cleveland Press* "What Price Glory" trophy in 1925. Van Oeyen's journalistic career enabled him to make acquaintance with many of the sports stars of the 1900s to 1930s. *Western Reserve Historical Society.*

Grange, Tilden, and Jones were enshrined in the pantheon of heroes formerly reserved for those named Washington, Grant, Lincoln, and Pershing.

Van Oeyen's images of the baseball greats of the 1920s were only part of his vast output of photos chronicling a variety of local sports ranging from hockey to football, track and field, and even boat and airplane racing. His work accurately mirrored the tremendous explosion in sports that took place in the interwar years. It was an explosion that catered to the spectator, and was part and parcel of the speculative business fever of the 1920s. Inventing and/or marketing sports for public consumption was as much a part of the American economic scene as selling shares in RCA or land in Florida. Ballyhoo, business, and bust were part of American life in the period from 1920 to the eve of World War II, and nowhere was this better represented than in the field of sports. Sports meant money and prestige, not only to businessmen and promoters but to the ordinary citizen who both admired the Olympian feats of the athletes and saw in their salaries and public recognition a model and means for advancement. Nowhere was this model more meaningful than in the immigrant neighborhoods and racial ghettos housing those new to American and/or urban society.

Cleveland changed dramatically during the interwar period. Its economy peaked in 1929 and then was leveled by the ensuing Depression. At times, one-third of the city's workforce was unemployed. Noted capitalist Cyrus Eaton commented that Cleveland was hurt more severely than any other city in the country. Only the prosperity of war would redeem its economic promise. Its population also changed, shifting to new suburban areas such as Cleveland Heights and Shaker Heights in the 1920s and, because of the economic setback, shrinking by over 22,000 during the 1930s. The composition of the population also shifted. With the restriction of immigration from Europe, African-Americans came north to provide a larger portion of

One of Louis Van Oeyen's more candid photos captures Yankee legend Lou Gehrig playing with a yo-yo prior to a Yankees-Indians game, 12 June 1932. *Western Reserve Historical Society.*

Cleveland Indian shortstop Ray Chapman, ca. 1919. *Cleveland Press Collection, Cleveland State University.*

the city's workforce, increasing in number from slightly over 8,400 in 1910 to over 84,000 in 1940.

Sports also changed in Cleveland during this period. The city had begun the post–World War I era with only one major professional sport, baseball, but by the beginning of the next world conflict, strong roots existed for several others, most notably football, hockey, and basketball. By 1940 its single 27,000-seat baseball stadium had been augmented by a gigantic 80,000-seat municipal park on the lakefront, as well as a new 10,000-seat indoor arena designed to accommodate the growing sports of hockey and basketball. Dozens of amateur ball diamonds located in Gordon, Edgewater, Brookside, and Garfield parks, among other locations, dotted the landscape by the end of the 1930s, as did a growing number of golf courses, both public and private, and tennis courts. The business boom of the 1920s gave rise to many of these new sports enterprises—it is a testament to their strength and to the increased social and economic value of recreation that many managed to survive the Depression that followed.

Baseball set the scene of sports both locally and nationally in the 1920s. Its image, tarnished by the Chicago "Black Sox" scandal of 1919, improved triumphantly during the next decade because of the feats of players such as Babe Ruth. It didn't matter that Ruth wasn't a member of the hometown team; his appearance at venues such as League Park attracted crowds and adulation. Clevelanders admired

Ruth, even though they had little use for losses to his Yankees. The fact that he hit his 500th home run at their park was a matter of consequence for local citizens. The fact that Ruth, coming from a deprived and hardly angelic childhood, arrived barely sober at some of his contests and was less than the physically ideal athlete did little to dampen hero worship.

Fortunately, Clevelanders could also admire their own baseball team at the same time. Under the leadership of Tris Speaker, the Indians won the 1920 American League pennant and then went on to defeat the Brooklyn Dodgers in a best-of-nine World Series. An unassisted triple play by Bill Wambsganss, the first Series grand-slam home run by Elmer Smith, and three pitching victories by Stanley Coveleski added luster to the win. Only the death (resulting from being hit by a pitch) of the team's shortstop, Ray Chapman, earlier in the season dampened the

Wade Park Horseshoe Club members at Wade Park, July 1938. Recreational activities such as pitching horseshoes provided relaxation and time for socialization for many Clevelanders during the Great Depression. *Cleveland Press Collection, Cleveland State University.*

RAYMOND JOHNSON "RAY" CHAPMAN (15 Jan. 1892–17 Aug. 1920), an exceptional shortstop for the Cleveland Indians between 1912 and 1920, was the only major-leaguer to die after being hit by a pitched ball. Chapman led the league in sacrifice hits three times, and set a major-league record with 67 sacrifices in 1917. On 16 Aug. 1920, Chapman was beaned by the Yankees' Carl Mays at the New York Polo Grounds. He died 12 hours later. The Indians dedicated the season to him, and went on to win their first World Series.

STANLEY ANTHONY "STAN" COVELESKI (13 July 1889–20 Mar. 1984) was a pitcher for the Cleveland Indians from 1916 to 1924. Famous for his brilliant control (and his spitball), Coveleski won 20 or more games a season from 1917 to 1921, winning a career-high 24 games in 1920. In the 1920 World Series, he led the Indians to three victories over Brooklyn, and in each game yielded only five hits. Elected to the Baseball Hall of Fame in 1969, Coveleski won 215 games and lost 141 during his 14-year career, compiling an exceptionally low 2.88 earned run average.

World Series heroes Stanley Coveleski (*left***) and Bill Wambsganss during the 1920 championship season.** *Western Reserve Historical Society.*

ELMER JOHN SMITH (21 Sept. 1892–3 Aug. 1984) played outfield for the Cleveland Indians from 1914 to 1921 and was noted for hitting the first grand-slam home run in World Series history, at Dunn Field (League Park) in 1920. In his 10-year career in the major leagues from 1914 to 1925, Smith played with the Cleveland, Washington, Boston, and New York clubs in the American League and Cincinnati in the National League. His best years were with Cleveland when he hit .321 in 1914 and .316 in 1920.

spirit of the victory. That tragedy in August served to harden the team's resolve to win the pennant. It also showed just how important baseball had become in the city—Chapman's funeral at St. John's Cathedral was reportedly the largest in Cleveland's history.

The Series victory proved the high point for the team for almost the next three decades. The Indians continued to play good baseball during the 1920s and 1930s, usually finishing in the first division and even achieving second place in 1921 and 1926. The lack of field success did not greatly diminish the crowds during the 1920s, however, and the team seemed a good business proposition—so good, in fact, that it was purchased from its Chicago owners by a group of Clevelanders. The new owners included former mayor and United States Secretary of War Newton D. Baker; old-line businessman John Sherwin, Jr.; Baker's law partner, Joseph Hostetler; and two sets of brothers: Charles and Alva Bradley, and Oris Paxton and Mantis James Van Sweringen. Alva Bradley was one of the major shipbuilders on the Great Lakes, and the Van Sweringens were in the midst of a storybook career that included building the Cleveland Union Terminal, developing Shaker Heights, and operating one of the nation's largest railroad empires. The local syndicate, which represented every level of business, society, and entrepreneurial activity, paid $975,000 for the franchise, and in doing so testified to the blue-chip status of baseball as an investment. Local ownership, of course, ensured that the Indians would once again be a "civic" as well as a business enterprise.

The new owners would never see their investment pay off in the currency of a World Series victory. The best they could settle for was a second-place finish in 1940, a year in which everyone expected the team to win the pennant, but during which an ongoing squabble between manager Oscar Vitt and his leading players, referred to as the "Cry Babies," served to undermine playing ability. Two major events did occur during the tenure of the new owners, however: the first was the construction of a new stadium on the lakefront, the second the acquisition of one of the greatest pitchers the game had ever seen.

Cleveland's new lakefront stadium was unlike any of the professional athletic

Elmer Smith (*left*) sits with Emil "Dutch" Levsen, ca. 1921. *Western Reserve Historical Society.*

Charlie Jamieson, Bill Wambsganss, and Tris Speaker score on a home run during the 1920 World Series, 10 October 1920. *Western Reserve Historical Society.*

fields ever built in the city. It was not a privately funded project, like the ballparks built by traction baron Frank Robison, which had been planned, in part, to increase use of his street railway lines. The new park was a municipal enterprise financed by a $2.5 million bond issue passed by the voters in 1928. The construction of a "Municipal Stadium," which had been advocated as early as 1900, marked a watershed in the general civic view of sports. City officials, in this case led by city manager William R. Hopkins, viewed sports as an economic benefit for the city. A city-owned facility would generate rental revenues from sports teams. Moreover, and more important, in the views espoused in the 1920s, a large, modern facility would attract conventions and other programs to Cleveland, which in turn would feed other aspects of the "service" economy. Despite cost overruns and setbacks caused

The 1920 WORLD SERIES marked the first postseason trip to the championships for the Cleveland Indians. Playing against the Brooklyn Dodgers in a best-of-9 playoff, the Indians dropped 2 of the first 3 games in Brooklyn, but returned to League Park in Cleveland and won 4 straight to capture the championship. Highlights include pitcher Stan Coveleski's 3 victories (3–1, 5–1, 3–0) and the amazing fifth game, which saw 3 World Series "firsts" recorded: the first home run by a pitcher (Jim Bagby), the first grand slam (by Elmer Smith), and the first unassisted triple play, by Bill (Wamby) Wambsganns.

JOSEPH WHEELER "JOE" SEWELL (9 Oct. 1898–6 Mar. 1990) was the Cleveland Indians shortstop who replaced Ray Chapman after Chapman's death during the 1920 season. Playing for the Indians from 1920 to 1930, Sewell batted a career average of .312 in his 14 major-league seasons, hitting a career-high .353 in 1926. Amazingly, he struck out only 114 times in 7,132 at-bats, and in 1929 played 115 games without a strikeout. In 1925 and 1929, he struck out only 4 times each year. Sewell was inducted into the Baseball Hall of Fame in 1977.

by the Depression, the stadium was completed on July 1, 1931. However, it would be another year before the Indians would play their first game there, and sixteen years before they would shift their entire season to the new park. Designed not specifically for baseball but as a venue for a multitude of sporting and nonsporting events, it elicited complaints from patrons more accustomed to the close confines of League Park. Also, its overwhelming size was wasted on the smaller crowds that viewed baseball on weekdays.

One attraction certain to increase crowd size during the 1930s was the appearance of Bob Feller, whose pitching skills brought national attention to the Cleveland team. In his major-league start, at age seventeen, on August 23, 1936, Feller struck out fifteen St. Louis Browns, one KO short of the American League record. Three weeks later he struck out seventeen Philadelphia Athletics. Born on a farm, young and clean-cut, Feller was exactly what was needed to enhance the all-American image of the game and to launch the Cleveland franchise into an exciting new era. Selected to pitch the first night game at the stadium, on June 27, 1939, Feller struck out thirteen Detroit Tigers during a one-hit shutout. Over 53,000 fans viewed the event. The following year he opened the season with a no-hitter, the first opening-day no-hitter in the history of the game.

Feller's success, along with that of fellow hurler Mel Harder, and the earlier championship of the 1920 Indians created great pride among Clevelanders in their team. Ironically, the talent of the young pitcher from Iowa, and the world champion team had few actual links to the city. In the 1860s when the Forest City nine played and won a game, it really did represent the athletic skills of at least certain of the citizens of Cleveland. But with the professionalization of the game in the 1870s, few players could be expected to have had their origins in the city they represented. Yet fan loyalty was undiminished. It was, of course, enhanced if there was some local connection, such as Ray Chapman's marriage to a local woman, Kathleen Daly. However, the determining factor for fan loyalty was an exciting team and, above all, a victorious team. The owners of professional baseball teams knew their profits would rise and fall with the tides of excitement and victory. Other sporting entrepreneurs would learn to heed this universal lesson as they tried to introduce Clevelanders to other sports in the interwar period.

Like baseball, these new entries into the consumer market of organized professional sport had amateur origins. Of those that gained vogue in Cleveland and the nation in the 1920s, football, despite its later popularity, had perhaps the most unpromising beginnings.

Hall of Fame Indians shortstop Joe Sewell takes a breather on the bench in April 1928. *Cleveland Press Collection, Cleveland State University.*

Indians Manager Oscar Vitt hits ground balls in April 1938. *Cleveland Press Collection, Cleveland State University.*

The ancestry of football is far more ancient than that of baseball. As related earlier, games involving the passing or moving of a ball through a goal were included in medieval town contests. As early as the days of the Jamestown settlement, men on the American continent may have been playing games involving an air-filled bladder. By 1875 Harvard and Yale competed in a "football" match that was part rugby and part soccer. The success of this one contest led to the creation, in 1876, of the Intercollegiate Football Association, with Princeton, Harvard, Yale, and Columbia as members.

Not until the 1880s, under the leadership of Walter Camp, did the "modern" form of American football begin to emerge, and not until the twentieth century did plays such as the forward pass become an approved part of the game, and new rules mitigate the death and injury once caused by mass running formations such as the flying wedge.

During the formative period of football, the game was associated almost entirely with colleges, in particular the Ivy League schools of the East. Despite its often bloody nature, football was a prestige game. The fictional dime-novel adventures of Frank Merriwell, a star Ivy League athlete during the late nineteenth century, vividly portrayed the manliness and class cachet associated with collegiate sports, particularly football. It was with these overtones, and not the beer and brawn attributes associated with the game some seven decades later, that football entered Cleveland.

Organized football came to the city in 1887 when a group of Central High

An airview of downtown Cleveland and Cleveland Municipal Stadium as it neared completion in 1931. *Cleveland Press Collection, Cleveland State University.*

School students defeated a Case School of Applied Science freshman team. However, interest in the game languished until the 1890s, when increasing newspaper coverage of East Coast college contests, and the experience brought back to Cleveland by Ivy League graduates increased local football activity. The area's first all-high-school game occurred in 1890, when University School defeated Central High. As interest grew, competition continued to cross educational levels as Central and University schools played college teams fielded by Adelbert College (of Western Reserve University) and the Case School. The sport was fairly widespread among area high schools and colleges by 1895, and by 1900 stories about football practice and games at the various educational institutions regularly found their way into the sports pages.

The major problem with the emerging game of football in Cleveland was a lack of organization. In addition to a mismatched level of play in which colleges played high schools and vice versa, teams were sprinkled with "ringers" who received pay for their services. A series of governing bodies on the local, state, and national levels were established to bring order to the game as well as to other "academic" sports. The first of these was the Ohio Athletic Conference, formed in 1902. Two years

HOWARD EARL AVERILL (21 May 1902–17 Aug. 1983) was an exceptional hitter and centerfielder for the Cleveland Indians from 1929 to 1939. Averill hit a home run in his first major-league at-bat, the first AL player ever to do so. Career highlights included hitting 4 home runs in a doubleheader on 17 Sept. 1930, selection to the first AL all-star team in 1933 and 4 times thereafter, and a career home run total of 238, the highest in Indians history. Averill was elected to the Hall of Fame in 1975.

later, Cleveland-area high-school administrators organized the Athletic Senate. In 1907 the National Collegiate Athletic Association came into being, as did the Ohio High School Athletic Association. Each organization worked in its own way to establish eligibility rules and academic standards for play. Most important, following the lead taken by the AAU in noncollegiate track and field, the academic regulatory agencies strongly emphasized the amateur nature of school sports. The day of the ringer was supposedly over.

With major rule changes in 1912 that provided for four rather than three downs for retention of the ball, and the shortening of the field from 110 to 100 yards, a good portion of the modern game was in place, and the principal venue for public viewing of that game was the collegiate field. The great expansion of college football as a school-spirit sport honoring the reputation of the alma mater, and as a profitable business for the school, occurred at both the smaller colleges in Cleveland and major schools such as Ohio State University. In fact, Case School of Applied Science was on an almost equal footing with the larger state schools. Under the guidance of Frank Van Horn, it reigned as one of the state's major football powers from 1902 to 1911. A good football program pleased alumni, attracted business to the school, and enticed would-be students. During the years from 1920 to 1945, games played by Case, Western Reserve, John Carroll, and Baldwin Wallace attracted as much local fan attention as those played by such national powerhouses as Notre Dame. Notre Dame did have a special attraction for Clevelanders during the 1920s, however, as one of its "four horsemen," Don Miller, had ties to the city. His brother, Ray T. Miller, would become the city's mayor and the leader of its Democratic Party in the 1930s. In Cleveland, as elsewhere, one of the institutional acknowledgments of the potential of football was a gradual shift of control of the game from the players, interested faculty, and alumni who had put the teams together, to the school administration. This shift occurred at Western Reserve in 1919, but was delayed at Case until 1947.

The economic possibilities of the game did not escape the notice of entrepreneurs—even the first game between Case and Reserve in 1891 had brought in $100 from 400 paying spectators. The problem for those entrepreneurs was partially in their source of inspiration. College football had, by the 1920s, already attracted many fans and therefore lessened the gate potential of any professional team. Then, too, baseball may have presented a problem in terms of absorbing a part of the audience, but careful scheduling of games could ensure that seasons would not overlap. Given the local college activity, it is no surprise that professional football came late to Cleveland and for nearly twenty years was unable to find a secure place

Indians star centerfielder Howard Earl Averill waits patiently on deck during a 1936 Indians game. *Western Reserve Historical Society.*

MELVIN L. "MEL" HARDER (15 Oct. 1909–   ) pitched for the Cleveland Indians from 1928 to 1947. He compiled 223 career victories, second only to Bob Feller on the Indians' all-time win list, and pitched in 582 games, more than any other Cleveland player. "Chief" Harder led the Indians in season victories four times (1934, 1935, 1937, and 1938) and played in the All-Star game four consecutive years (1934–37). He served as interim manager for the Indians at the end of the 1961 and 1962 seasons, after Jimmy Dykes and Mel McGaha, respectively, were fired.

in the local sports economy. Although professional football was played by teams throughout northeastern Ohio beginning in 1903, it was not until 1916 that an attempt was made to introduce a play-for-pay game in Cleveland.

The guiding force behind the city's first professional team was Gene W. "Peggy" Parratt. Parratt was not new to the field of sports for money. A star baseball and football player for Case Institute, he was dropped from Case athletics in 1905 when it was discovered he was playing for cash on Sundays with a local athletic club under the pseudonym Jimmy Murphy. Parratt joined with sports promoter Herman Schleman to form the Cleveland Indians football team in 1916. Although the Indians defeated the renowned Carlisle Indians in their opening game and accumulated an 8-3-and-1 record, the team was a fiscal failure and it disbanded.

In 1919 sports promoter Jimmy O'Donnell joined with former East Technical High School and Notre Dame football star Stanley B. Cofall in establishing the Cleveland Tigers (sometimes called the Cleveland Indians) as part of the Ohio League. In 1920, O'Donnell joined with other pro team owners at Ralph Hay's Hupmobile Agency in Canton in a meeting that led to the creation of the American Professional Football Association (which would later become the National Football League). In obtaining a franchise for the Tigers in the new league, O'Donnell would allow future Clevelanders the satisfaction of knowing that their city was part of the beginning of modern professional football in the United States.

The honor was dubious, however, for the team lasted barely two years. Winning only one game during the 1920 season, the franchise secured the services of two future hall-of-famers, Joe Guyon and Jim Thorpe, for the next season. With Thorpe injured early in the season, the Tigers again ended up with a losing record. Matters were so bad that O'Donnell asked permission from the league to suspend operations in 1922. His request was approved, but when he was unable to come up with the league's annual $1,000 guarantee, the franchise was canceled.

The litany of poor performance and financial collapse continued through the remainder of the decade. In 1923, jeweler Samuel Deutsch bought the Cleveland NFL franchise and continued the team under the name the Indians. It finished fifth in the twenty-team league. Determined to ensure a winning season, Deutsch next bought a championship team, the Canton Bulldogs, for Cleveland. He paid $2,500 for the team, which had won championships in 1922 and 1923. Despite its victorious seasons, the Canton team had lost $13,000 in 1923, and future play was about to be suspended by its management. Money seemed to be the answer, and under the tutelage of coach Guy Chamberlin (a future hall-of-famer), in 1924 the Cleveland

Indians pitcher Mel Harder warms up at Cleveland Municipal Stadium in 1938. Harder won 223 games in 20 seasons as an Indian from 1928 to 1947. *Western Reserve Historical Society.*

ROBERT W. A. "BOB" FELLER (3 Nov. 1918–   ) pitched for the Cleveland Indians from 1936 to 1956, and over his career established himself as the best Indians pitcher ever. Signed on by the Indians as a 17-year-old schoolboy, "Rapid Robert" threw 3 no-hitters and 12 one-hitters for the Tribe, and led the American League in strikeouts 7 times and wins 6 times. The Indians' all-time leader with 266 career victories, 2,581 strikeouts, and 46 shutouts, Feller retired after the 1956 season. He was inducted into the Baseball Hall of Fame in 1962.

Bulldogs brought Cleveland its first professional football championship. Apparently success was not everything, because in 1925 Deutsch sold the team to Herb Brandt of the Brandt food company. The Bulldogs went on to a disastrous season, finishing in twelfth place. Matters were so bad that the 1926 season was suspended.

Deutsch and Brandt certainly had every reason to have expected things to go

Legendary Indians pitcher Bob Feller kicks through his windup, ca. late 1930s. Feller threw three no-hitters and won 266 games in eighteen seasons with the Tribe. *Western Reserve Historical Society.*

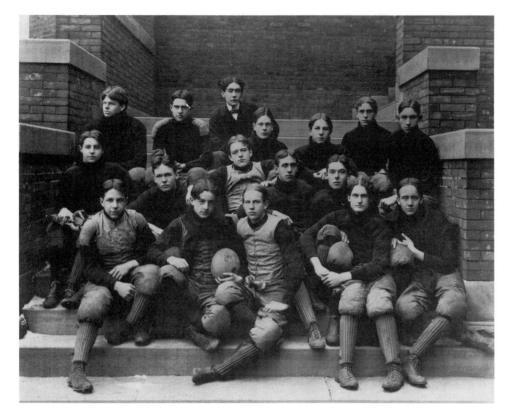

better than they did, for in 1925–26 professional football began, at last, to catch on and gain popular attention. This was almost entirely a result of the Chicago Bears' signing of Red Grange of the University of Illinois in 1925. The most widely recognized college star of the early 1920s, Grange brought a much-needed touch of class to the rough-and-tumble world of early professional football. A national tour by Grange and the Bears helped spread the popularity of the game. Cleveland promoters, however hard they tried, seemed unable to capitalize on this trend.

The growing potential of the national game led to the establishment of a rival league, the American Football League, in 1926. Cleveland quickly entered a team in the AFL. The Cleveland Panthers were the creation of asphalt company president Charles X. Zimmerman (who also served as vice-president of the nine-team league). Drawing talent from the now-moribund Bulldogs, as well as recruiting former college stars such as Al Michaels and Cookie Cunningham, the team jumped off to a most promising start. Its first game was played before 22,000 spectators at the stadium at a local amusement park, Luna Park. A reported claimed it was the largest crowd ever to have witnessed football in the city, and gave the team the ultimate compliment, saying that the Panthers "looked like a real collegiate eleven." Within a month, however, typical crowds had dwindled to 1,000 per game. The decline in the Panthers' fortunes continued when the team, while in Philadelphia preparing for a game, was sued for $1,000 by the Stearns Advertising Company. Unable to pay, the franchise was placed in receivership, the team was broken up, and the players were left stranded in Philadelphia. Sensing some salvage possibilities among the debris of the AFL franchise, NFL Bulldogs owner Herb Brandt signed most of the Panther players and managed to get them back to Cleveland in time for at least one NFL Bulldog game to be played during the 1926 season.

By 1927 the Bulldogs were back in action. Again Sam Deutsch was among the owners, who also included Max Rosenblum, Herb Brandt, Harold Gould, and dentist Clinton C. Winfrey. Cleveland tried anew to buy its way to a championship,

FRANK R. VAN HORN (7 Feb. 1872–1 Aug. 1933) was a renowned and widely published mineralogist and geologist at Case School of Applied Science who served as head of the school's athletic association for 26 years. Assuming office in 1900, Van Horn quickly gave structure to the association's poorly organized administration and policies. Deemed "the Father of Case Athletics," Van Horn saved the football program and encouraged athletic endeavors for the student body.

first by signing native Clevelander and University of Michigan star quarterback Benny Friedman, and then by purchasing an entire team, the former 1926 Kansas City Cowboys (a group described as "raw-boned, rangy lads"). Friedman, a product of Glenville High School and the star athlete of the local Jewish community, seemed certain to boost attendance at Bulldog games. The attempt failed, and the team known as "Benny Friedman's Cleveland Bulldogs" ended up in fourth place with an 8-4-and-1 record. At this point, Deutsch had evidently had enough, and he apparently sold the team to Detroit in 1928—the Detroit Wolverines roster for that year included twelve former Bulldogs. When the Wolverines subsequently went on the market and were sold to Tim Mara, his 1929 New York Giants included eight former Bulldogs. Cleveland may not have been able to sustain a football team, but at least it helped supply players to teams that would later become legendary.

The almost comical nature of the history of professional football franchises in Cleveland during the 1920s can be attributed largely to the fact that college and even good-quality high-school ball was generally available. At least four college teams—Western Reserve, Case, John Carroll, and Baldwin Wallace—were always active. Given the high regard in which college ball was held in relation to the professional game, it is not surprising that patronage of the local athletic gridiron dug deeply into the potential revenues of any professional team. Indeed, even imported college games—for instance, the Notre Dame versus Navy contest of 1939—drew better than professional ball. That particular game, held in Municipal Stadium, drew 81,000 spectators. Then, too, the professional teams had heavy financial burdens to bear—franchise fees, travel costs, and salaries—while amateur college ball had the support of a college budget. The competition was uneven. It would take a larger, more affluent city to support professional football. Crowds and profits would not characterize local professional football until the 1950s.

The Depression dampened most entrepreneurial activity, even in sports, and it was not until 1936 that Cleveland investors again tried to organize a professional football team in the city. That effort, spearheaded by former Ohio State University fullback Damon "Buzz" Wetzel, and financed by a group that included local attorney Homer Marshman, resulted in the establishment of the Cleveland Rams as a member of the American Football League. The team finished second in the league, but the season was still a financial disaster. Making a bad situation worse, members of the Boston team, scheduled to confront the Rams in the playoffs, refused to play because they had not been paid.

The Rams moved to the National Football League in the following year, with owners and stockholders putting up the $10,000 franchise fee and raising $55,000 to

Famed mineralogist and Case Institute professor Frank "The Count" Van Horn in 1931. *Case Western Reserve University Archives.*

BENJAMIN "BENNY" FRIEDMAN (18 Mar. 1905–23 Nov. 1982) was a star quarterback in college and professional football during the 1920s and 1930s. The son of Jewish immigrants, Friedman led Glenville High School to the city championship in 1922, and was a two-time consensus All-American in three seasons at the University of Michigan (1924, 1925, and 1926). He played for the National Football League Cleveland Bulldogs in 1927, the Detroit Wolverines in 1928, the New York Giants from 1929 to 1931, and the Brooklyn Dodgers from 1932 to 1934. A coach and athletic director in his later years, Friedman was elected to the College Football Hall of Fame in 1952.

capitalize the club. Between 1937 and 1942, the team never finished higher than third place. By 1941, it was on the market again. Daniel F. Reeves and Frederick Levy purchased the franchise for about $100,000, but, with a war on, they never recovered their investment while the Rams played in Cleveland. The 1943 season was canceled, and the 1944 season turned out poorly. In 1945, with Bob Waterfield as quarterback, the Rams won the NFL Western Division title and went on to win the championship by defeating the Washington Redskins. Still the club was in debt. In 1946 the team would leave the city when a competitor, the Cleveland Browns, playing in the All American Conference, threatened to split the limited gate.

The popular conception of the 1920s as a period of risky, get-rich-quick

Cleveland Bulldog quarterback Benny Friedman, pictured with son Leslie in 1952. *Cleveland Press Collection, Cleveland State University.*

A Western Reserve player looks for the open field in a game against Case Institute, 28 November 1941. Local college rivalries consistently drew large crowds to the Stadium. *Case Western Reserve University Archives.*

schemes seems to be confirmed in the story of Cleveland's attempts to establish a lasting professional football team. Even more typical of the period is the history of professional basketball. Taking what was originally envisioned as a character-building amateur sport, local entrepreneurs used imagination and ballyhoo to create a sometimes viable game in the city. As early as 1909, the Buffalo Germans, a touring professional team, appeared in Cleveland, where they played the Columbias. Outclassed, the Columbias were humiliated by a 70 to 22 score. In the 1920s the touring New York Celtics came to Cleveland to play in the new Public Hall. They attracted near-capacity crowds in the 12,000-seat facility during the winter of 1922–23. Basketball seemed a likely candidate for investors seeking to capitalize on the new spectator interest in sports.

The same potential was apparent throughout the country, and in 1925 the first national professional league, the American Basketball League, was formed. Not only did it provide a structure for scheduling games, but it also standardized the often divergent sets of rules then in operation around the country and imposed its own version of baseball's reserve clause to keep players from moving from team to team. Cleveland, led by clothier Max Rosenblum (who would later try his hand at football), entered the league with its own team, the Cleveland Rosenblums. Immediately successful, the Rosenblums won the first league championship in 1925. However, when the New York Celtics entered the league the following year, every other team was thoroughly outclassed. Winning game after game, the Celtics drove attendance figures down, as fans of local teams gave up hope. Three teams collapsed under the Celtic onslaught. Only when the league broke up the Celtics in 1928, distributing their players to the remaining teams, did competition become viable. The Rosenblums, richer by three Celtic players, again won championships in the next two years. The onset of the Depression, however, drove revenues down, and by 1930 the Rosenblums withdrew from the league, continuing to play only touring

ROBERT "BOB" WATERFIELD (26 July 1920–25 Mar. 1983) was a star quarterback for the 1945 Cleveland and 1946–52 Los Angeles Rams, and led the Cleveland team to the NFL Championship as a rookie in 1945 while garnering NFL MVP honors. Waterfield, who played college ball at UCLA, was a punter and placekicker and played defense as well, intercepting 20 passes in his 8 NFL seasons. During his career, Waterfield completed 813 of 1,617 passes (50.3%) for 11,849 yards and 98 touchdowns. A 3-time All-NFL selection, Waterfield was elected to the Hall of Fame in 1965.

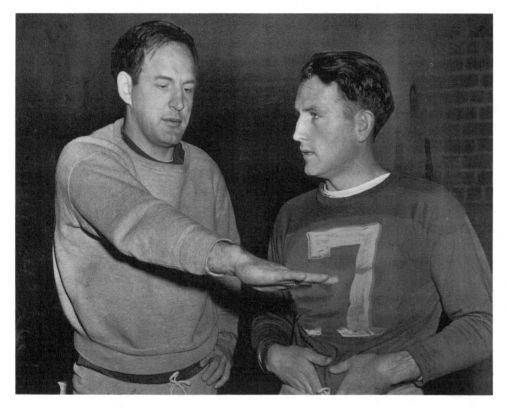

Bob Waterfield of the Cleveland Rams discusses plays with coach Jim Benton before Cleveland's 15-14 championship victory over the Washington Redskins on 16 December 1945. *Cleveland Press Collection, Cleveland State University.*

Cleveland Rams quarterback Bob Waterfield led the Rams to a National Football League championship in 1945 while garnering the league's Most Valuable Player award as a rookie. *Cleveland Press Collection, Cleveland State University.*

pro teams. Not until late in the decade would local entrepreneurs again try to introduce league basketball to Cleveland.

Ironically, the third new team sport introduced to Cleveland in the 1920s, and the one which, at first glance, would seem to be least likely to survive, did manage to make it through the financially troubled 1930s. Ice hockey was a Canadian import, first having been played in an organized fashion in that country in the 1860s. The game's antecedents can be traced to shinny, a field game played on foot with a ball and sticks. Shinny was reportedly played in Cleveland during the 1830s. In the Canadian climate it could be expected that shinny would find itself transmuted into a fast-paced game played on ice by men on skates. The rough and often violent nature of the game was apparent from the beginning. Fights at the first indoor game in Montreal in 1875 caused women spectators to flee from the stands.

MAX ROSENBLUM (5 Dec. 1877–5 Sept. 1953), Cleveland clothing magnate, was the owner of the Rosenblums-Celtics professional basketball team and was known as the father of sandlot baseball in Cleveland. In 1925 he helped to establish the American Basketball League. His team, the Cleveland Rosenblums, managed by I. S. (Nig) Rose, captured the 1925–26 championship. After signing former New York Celtic players, the team again was league champion in 1928–29 and 1929–30, though it folded later in 1930. Rosenblum was also a founder of the Cleveland Amateur Baseball Association and sponsored many sandlot teams.

Informal games of ice hockey were probably played in Cleveland as early as the 1890s, but not until 1929 was the professional game introduced to the city. Just before the stock market collapse, Harry "Happy" Holmes, a retired Canadian goalie, formed a team named the Cleveland Indians. It took $20,000 to get the team going, and Holmes was determined to see it survive despite worsening economic times. Playing at the Elysium ice rink at Euclid Avenue and East 107th Street, the Indians were a member of the minor International Hockey League. A first-rate promoter, Holmes touted his team as a diversion from the then faltering economy. Despite a lack of training, the Indians won the league championship in 1929–30. From this peak, Holmes's team slipped steadily, until it finished in last place in 1933–34. By this time the irrepressible Holmes had run out of money. Seeking to keep the team alive, he found a new backer in Albert C. Sutphin of the Braden-

Cleveland clothier and sports entrepreneur Max Rosenblum speaks into the microphone at the Stadium 14 July 1935. Rosenblum, known as the father of sandlot baseball in Cleveland, promoted a spectrum of amateur sports. *Western Reserve Historical Society.*

HAROLD "HAPPY" HOLMES (15 April 1889–27 June 1941), a retired Canadian goalie, gained a franchise in the International League and formed the Cleveland Indians hockey team in 1929. Playing at the Elysium, the team drew well during the 1929–30 season and won the league championship. A decline in the standings and in paid attendance during the next four years forced Holmes to sell the Indians to businessman Albert C. "Al" Sutphin in 1934. The team was rechristened the Cleveland Barons when it joined the new American Hockey League in 1936.

Sutphin Ink Corporation. A former goalie (for Central High School) and boxing commissioner, Sutphin was the consummate sports promoter.

As new owner, president, and treasurer of the franchise, Sutphin renamed the team the Falcons in 1934 and began a rebuilding program. The team improved, and in 1936 it became a charter member of the new minor-league circuit, the American Hockey League. To provide a better site for home games, Sutphin built the Cleveland Arena in 1937 and, after conducting a public contest for suggestions, renamed the team the Cleveland Barons. While the team played well and drew substantial crowds, it was undoubtedly Sutphin's arena that ensured its survival. In addition to hosting Barons home games, the facility was the site of Ice Follies performances, rodeos, high school basketball contests, and even concerts. It was hosting 330 events annually by 1940. Sutphin, unlike the owners of Cleveland's early football fran-

Former Cleveland Indians hockey team owner Harry Holmes and Al Sutphin (*with shovel*) at the groundbreaking for the Cleveland Arena in 1937. *Cleveland Press Collection, Cleveland State University.*

The Cleveland Indians hockey team en route to a 4-3 victory over Pittsburgh, ca. 1930. *Western Reserve Historical Society.*

chises, knew the secret of survival for new sports in the 1930s—diversity of investment.

The rise of professional sports as spectator entertainment during the 1920s and 1930s did not necessarily signal a consequent decline in amateur organized sports. On the contrary, the 1920s in Cleveland saw a blossoming of amateur competition, on the scholastic as well as the nonscholastic level. In both areas players and teams competed not only for the pure joy of the game, but to emulate their heroes in the professional ranks. And in both areas, entrepreneurial gain was often an implicit part of the contest.

The position of football in Cleveland-area colleges has already been noted. Next to that activity, basketball was the second most popular local collegiate sport. By the 1930s, the four football rivals Western Reserve, John Carroll, Case, and Baldwin Wallace had entered into an informal "Big Four" basketball rivalry. By this time the colleges played among themselves, and the earlier practice of scheduling games with noncollegiate teams had been dropped. Competitive college basketball in Cleveland during this period was a men's game. However, the area schools did have noncompetitive intramural games for women. Adhering to guidelines established by the National Section on Women's Athletics of the American Physical Education Association, women's basketball stressed exercise and athleticism rather than competition. Games were governed by "girls' rules," which led to a slower, less arduous game. The concept of gentility as a governing rule for sports suitable for females was therefore very much in evidence when local collegiate women took to the basketball courts. A variety of "scientific" arguments relating to women's physical capabilities (often focusing on the possible damage to reproductive systems that might be caused by strenuous activity) served to keep girls' rules in force for many years to come.

The most amazing expansion of scholastic sports during the interwar period took place on the high-school level. Two factors tended to account for the growth. Most critical was the increase in the high-school population. When organized sports

ALBERT C. SUTPHIN (11 Apr. 1894–25 June 1974), cofounder of the Braden-Sutphin Ink Co., was the initial owner of the Cleveland Barons hockey team. He bought the International League Cleveland Indians in 1934 from Harry Holmes and renamed the team the Cleveland Falcons. In 1937 he affiliated his renamed Barons with the American Hockey League. Also in 1937, Sutphin built the Cleveland Arena. Hailed as an "All-Sport Palace," the $1.5 million, 10,000-seat facility at 3717 Euclid Ave. was the home of the Barons. In the 1940s the Arena hosted over 300 entertainment and sports events a year, including ice shows, rodeos, high-school, college, and professional basketball, track meets, and boxing matches, including the championship bout on 24 June 1947 in which Jimmy Doyle died. Sutphin, known as "the man in the red necktie," sold the Arena and the Barons in 1949 (the obsolete building was demolished in 1977). A philanthropist, he donated $10,000 to the Cleveland Baseball Federation prior to his death in 1974.

first began to appear in Cleveland's schools in the late nineteenth century, relatively few students continued on to the high-school level. Schools such as Central High resembled colleges more than modern high schools, with classical curricula and exclusive networks of clubs and societies. As the city's population exploded after 1890, high-school attendance increased and the public schools became more "public." As this occurred, a host of private high schools, including University and Hawken for men and Hathaway Brown and Laurel for women, were established in order to preserve the upper-class standards that had once held sway at public

Al Sutphin on the phone in 1947. Sutphin's Cleveland Arena, while hosting a variety of special events, was the home of the Cleveland Barons for three decades. *Cleveland Press Collection, Cleveland State University.*

Women exercising with Indian clubs, ca. 1935. Calisthenics for students were viewed as vital by school administrators as early as the 1860s. *Cleveland Press Collection, Cleveland State University.*

schools such as Central. The greatest increase in school attendance took place after the passage of the state's Bing Act in 1921, which made school mandatory until age eighteen. By the 1920s the students in all of these schools, both private and public, shared in the era's burgeoning interest in sports, and this provided the second factor for program growth. Proving one's prowess and emulating the hero of the day became possible on the school athletic field.

Athletic activity in Cleveland's schools had a long history. Superintendent Luther Oviatt had introduced physical training in the schools in the early 1860s—calisthenics and working with Indian clubs were viewed as healthful for both boys and girls. As field events and organized sports became more popular later in the century, they worked their way into the schools—informally at first, as groups of students played games among themselves, and then as officially supervised and sanctioned activities. School administrators saw athletic activity not only as healthful but as a means to build character. Later, the income from athletic events would contribute yet another reason for scholastic sports—even if a sport did not produce a profit, it usually offset the costs associated with the contests. And, as late-nineteenth-century high schools tended to view themselves as "junior" colleges, activities such as football made the comparison with the collegiate world even more effective.

As in college, football and basketball proved the most popular sports in the high schools. Although baseball was played, its prime season fell in the middle of the annual summer vacation. The first attempt to organize and control these scholastic sports was the creation of the Senate League in 1904. By the 1920s, its membership comprised Central, Collinwood, East, East Technical, Glenville, John Adams, Lincoln, South, West, and West Technical high schools. In 1936 the senate was renamed the Cleveland Senate and was expanded to include three new public high schools: John Hay, John Marshall, and James Ford Rhodes, as well as four parochial schools: Benedictine, Cathedral Latin, Holy Name, and St. Ignatius, which had previously played in the Catholic League. At the same time an East and West Senate were created to enhance competition—the winners of sports titles in either senate would play in a final city championship. The interest in these championships can be gauged by the fact that after 1937 the East-West Senate championship was played as the city's annual Thanksgiving Charity Football Game, scheduled in the cavernous confines of the Municipal Stadium. This charity game had first been played in 1931 to raise funds for Christmas donations. Before the institution of the split senate, the competing teams were selected by a committee of scholastic officials.

The level of greatest amateur sports activity in Cleveland after World War I, however, was not in the colleges or high schools but in the area of sponsored amateur teams. Beginning in the early 1900s, businesses began to see a great promotional value in sponsoring amateur teams in baseball, basketball, and, eventually, football. The cost to the business was the price of the uniforms and equipment. The payoff was having its name on the shirts or jerseys of the team members. Nothing says more about the growing popularity of sports in Cleveland than the fact that astute businessmen found that one of their best sources of advertisement was to be associated with a (they hoped) winning athletic team. The practice, of course, fell into a gray area between true amateurism and professionalism. However, the Amateur Athletic Union eventually approved of sponsorship of teams.

By the 1920s, sponsorship of athletic teams had expanded. A team might be supported by a consortium of neighborhood merchants and thus play as a representative of a district of the city or an ethnic group; others might be sponsored by churches, industries, and fraternal associations. Nowhere was the number of teams and sponsors greater than in amateur baseball. By 1910 so many teams were playing sandlot ball that the Cleveland Amateur Baseball Association was formed to organize them and oversee the rules. By the 1920s, teams were categorized in a series of classes ranging from E to AAA. Classes A to AAA were semiprofessional and formed the basis of minor-league baseball throughout the country. Each classification equated to a different skill level. The classes spanned dozens of leagues, including at least two industrial leagues, a bankers' league, and an indoor ball league. Diamonds proliferated and could be found in each of the city's municipal parks, as well as near factories that sponsored industrial league teams. Some of the most noted diamonds were located at Edgewater, Gordon, Brookside, and Washington parks. The natural amphitheater at Brookside Park held the largest crowd (100,000+) ever to see a baseball game in Cleveland when the local White Auto team defeated a team from Omaha for the national amateur championship. A panoramic photograph of the huge crowd was displayed for years in Brookside-area bars which catered to the sporting crowd.

Despite the "amateur" status of the players, members of the various teams and leagues moved about with great frequency. What rewards were offered to occasion team-jumping can only be left to speculation. Within the industrial leagues, the record of a team had much to do with the prestige of the employing institution, particularly in the sports-conscious 1920s. Retired machinists in Cleveland, for in-

FINAL INTER-CITY CHAMPIONSHIP GAME - WHITE AUTOS vs OMAHA LUXUS TEAM - BROOKSIDE STADIUM - OCT. 10, 1915
SCORE - 11 TO 6 IN FAVOR WHITE AUTOS - ATTENDANCE OVER 100,000

Brookside Park was one of many parks around the city with a baseball diamond. The field's natural amphitheater, however, made it an exceptional one, capable of holding record crowds. *Western Reserve Historical Society.*

stance, could reminisce about the "good old days" when an adept player could easily find a job in one factory or another by virtue of his skill on the diamond rather than his ability on the lathe or drill press.

Although the promotion of amateur baseball suffered when the Depression cut company and business expenditures for team supplies and sponsorship, the sandlots of the city continued to be busy. In 1921 the Cleveland Amateur Baseball Association became the Cleveland Baseball Federation. Under the tireless leadership of William T. Duggan and with the support of the city recreation department, amateur baseball was promoted as a means to combat juvenile delinquency. Yearly "amateur

The Torbenson Axle sandlot baseball team, ca. 1920. Sponsorship of amateur ballclubs ranged from churches to industries to fraternal organizations. *Cleveland Press Collection, Cleveland State University.*

days" gave support to the cause well past the beginning of the Depression. By the 1930s, Cleveland still had enough active amateur teams to be dubbed the "Sandlot Capital of the World." The extent of the game was enormous. During World War II, the city could claim 25,000 sandlot "veterans" serving in the United States armed forces.

Nonscholastic amateur basketball also proliferated during the interwar years. Again, business sponsorship played a large role in promoting the game—after all, it was relatively inexpensive to outfit a basketball team. All a business needed to provide were jerseys bearing the company name. No bats, gloves, or other paraphernalia were involved. The heights to which such company teams could ascend were epitomized by the Cleveland Rosenblums, who, as noted earlier, became one of the first member teams of the professional American Basketball League. Other teams played in the Muny Leagues supervised by the city of Cleveland. The growth of the amateur aspect of the sport prompted, as in baseball, the creation of a regulatory and oversight agency, the Greater Cleveland Basketball Commission, in 1929. By 1935 it oversaw play in a city that had over 1,000 amateur teams.

The remarkable involvement of women in basketball set it apart from the other amateur team sports in the post–World War I era. There was a women's amateur team in the city as early as 1918. This team, and others, played according to the men's rules, and thus they were not limited to the two-court game played by the intramurals in colleges. By the 1930s, several amateur and industrial women's basketball leagues were playing in the city. In that decade a team sponsored by Fisher Foods (the originator of a local "pigtail" league) was invited to Canada for the unofficial world series.

Somewhat surprisingly, nonscholastic amateur football also thrived in Cleveland during this period. The owners of the various professional franchises might have envied the carefree play of such teams. By the time of World War I, amateur teams sponsored by churches or athletic clubs began to give way to those sponsored by businesses. By the 1920s the Blepp Knits, Bartlett Drugs, Favorite Knits, and Langgereths Tailors dominated the amateur gridiron. They could only aspire to the success of teams such as those sponsored by a packing company in Green Bay, Wisconsin, or a Decatur, Illinois, corn products team that would move to Chicago and assume the nickname "Bears." Other teams, sponsored typically by a coalition of neighborhood interests, upheld neighborhood and ethnic pride. The Mohawks, a misleadingly named all-Italian team, won the city championship each year from 1914 to 1918.

The hopes of local entrepreneurs for making a fortune from sports, as well as the participation of citizens as both spectators and amateur players, indicated how well sports in Cleveland fit into the milieu of the 1920s, when that decade is characterized on the basis of its speculative economic trends and its extraordinary fascination with such heroes as Babe Ruth, Charles Lindbergh, and Tris Speaker. There were other, sometimes less recognized aspects of the social history of the 1920s and the Depression-era 1930s that were mirrored in sports. These centered around the development of a solid middle class, and around the aspirations of people outside the American mainstream.

Among the most visible sports-related manifestations of the growing middle class in Cleveland during the 1920s were the inroads it made into several sports once considered the purview of the well-monied elite in the city. In particular, golf became a more broadly based sport in the 1920s. Its rise in popularity was due in part to the aura of success it carried, as well as to its potential as a catalyst for business activity. Entertaining one's client at the golf club could spell success for an up-and-coming businessman.

The "Clark Munies," women's state champions in 1920, were one of many women's amateur basketball teams which, like men's teams, survived through business sponsorship. *Cleveland Press Collection, Cleveland State University.*

The growth of golf during the interwar period occurred at various levels. As the number of the very wealthy in Cleveland expanded, additional private country clubs suited to their means were created. As upper-middle-income businessmen became more numerous, other new clubs, of lesser status, came into being. And, at a lower socioeconomic level still, local government recognized the value of the game to its citizens and opened public courses.

At the upper end of the scale in Cleveland, clubs such as the Canterbury Golf Club (1921) and the Acacia Country Club (1923) were opened. The former grew out of the private University Club, and the latter initially had a membership limited to Masons. Neither, however, rivaled the old established Country Club. The growing

Women golfers at Shaker Heights Country Club in May 1926. During the interwar period, golf's growing popularity cut across class, gender, and economic lines. *Western Reserve Historical Society.*

WILLIAM ALBERT STINCHCOMB (5 June 1878–17 Jan. 1959) was the father and directing genius of the Cleveland Metroparks District created in 1917. He developed recreational and sports facilities, including picnic areas, shelterhouses, swimming beaches, and bridle and hiking trails in the parks, believing that contact with nature was essential to the well-being of urban dwellers. As the demand for public golf courses grew in the 1920s, Stinchcomb opened the first metropolitan course in the Rocky River Reservation.

upper-income suburb of Shaker Heights had its own club. The Shaker Heights Country Club had been established some years earlier (1913) in the area, thanks in large part to the Van Sweringens, who gave the club its land (they would also provide land to the Country Club to prompt its move to Pepper Pike in 1928). In doing so, they counted on the club being a key attraction to the development of their new suburb. Other clubs opened during the decade included the Chagrin Valley Club, Aurora Country Club, and Pepper Pike Country Club (1925). Additional golf courses opened at Columbia Hills (1928) and Manikiki (1929). The growth of golf in Cleveland, particularly at the country club level, paralleled a national trend. By 1929 there were 4,500 clubs in the United States.

At the opposite end of the golf spectrum were the public courses. In 1925 William Stinchcomb, the father of the Metroparks system, oversaw the opening of Metropolitan Number 1 in the Rocky River Reservation. The city of Cleveland operated a second public course. Founded before 1920, and initially situated at Woodland Hills Park, the facility was later moved to city land in Warrensville Township, where it became known as the Highland Park Golf Course. Eight clubs admitted the general public to their courses by 1930. The number of golf courses in the county increased to thirty-three by 1941, and consisted of sixteen private, fifteen semiprivate, and two public courses. Golf, now a sport of the upper-middle as well as the upper echelons of local society, weathered the Depression quite well.

Despite the celebrity of golfing greats such as Bobby Jones, the game still remained largely a participant sport. Tournaments did come to Cleveland. Before the end of World War II, area clubs had played host to four Western Opens, two U.S. Opens, one Women's Western Open, one Women's National Championship, one Cleveland Open, and a number of state championships. Prize monies were limited, usually to no more than $10,000 for the winner, and crowds were small and restrained.

Even the equine-centered sports—with the exception of riding to hounds—saw a slight blurring of class lines. Polo expanded, with a new nonprivate field being opened in the Chagrin Valley at Chagrin River Road and Kinsman Road in 1931. Set matches played under the auspices of the U.S. Polo Association's Central Circuit attracted surprising numbers of people. Although the nineteen games of the National Championships at Walter White's Circle W Farm in 1928 attracted a total attendance of only 8,000, crowds of 2,000 to 3,000 were common at afternoon games at the River Road field during weekends in the mid-1930s. Indoor polo began in 1922 and lasted into the 1930s, with competition among teams sponsored by businesses such as Fisher Foods as well as "private" teams such as that of Troop A, a

William Stinchcomb, the father of the city's extensive Metropark System. *Cleveland Press Collection, Cleveland State University.*

local National Guard cavalry unit made up, at one time, of members of some of the city's most prominent families. Such local teams also competed at indoor polo against college teams from Yale and Harvard. During one season during the 1930s, the indoor version of the game drew 54,000 spectators.

The premier equine-centered sport, harness racing, fell on hard times during the postwar period. Only the dogged determination of sportsmen such as Harry Devereux kept the sport alive. He felt it his duty to provide future leaders of society with racing skills. Devereux died in 1932, and the Grand Circuit harness races at the North Randall track ceased in 1938. An era of gentlemanly sportsmanship had passed. The harness races were eventually replaced with organized thoroughbred horse races, which would attract a new clientele to both the North Randall track and its sister Thistledown Race Track, which had been opened in the racing suburb in 1925.

Devereux lamented the demise of harness racing, blaming it on the increasing fascination with the automobile. He was perhaps correct, for a finely built racing car represented to Americans of the 1920s and 1930s many of the same attributes that Devereux and nineteenth-century racers saw in their horses. To either group of beholders, their respective idols had beauty and power (although one could argue that an auto could never have the animals' "grace") and the potential for improvement, for by breeding or tinkering one could produce a more successful product, be it horse or car.

However, in the mechanical age of the 1920s, Clevelanders were not so much fascinated by speed on the ground as by speed in the air. If the city can hold claim to a unique sporting contribution of its own, it was the total dominance of Cleveland, its businesses, and its citizens in holding, promoting, and attending one of the most popular sports events of the late 1920s and 1930s, the National Air Races. Originally held in Los Angeles in 1928, the races were brought to Cleveland in 1929, largely through the efforts of a group of businessmen led by Frederick C. Crawford of Thompson Products. His company, a manufacturer of valves and other parts for

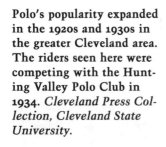

Polo's popularity expanded in the 1920s and 1930s in the greater Cleveland area. The riders seen here were competing with the Hunting Valley Polo Club in 1934. *Cleveland Press Collection, Cleveland State University.*

FREDERICK C. CRAWFORD (19 Mar. 1891–   ), maverick industrialist, civic leader, and philanthropist, was instrumental in bringing the National Air Races to Cleveland. Born in Watertown, Massachusetts, the Harvard-educated Crawford came to Cleveland, where he rose to become president of Thompson Products, later known as TRW. As president of the Air Races' sponsoring organization in Cleveland, Crawford created the "Thompson Trophy" in 1930, and his efforts helped to establish Cleveland as principal host city of the Air Races.

automobiles and aircraft, had a vested interest in seeing aviation prosper and become more popular. Although the races traveled to other cities, they came back to Cleveland in 1931, 1932, 1935, 1937, 1938, and 1939. The highlight of the multifaceted event was the Thompson Trophy Race, a fifty-five-mile contest on a closed course demarcated by pylons. Featuring flyers such as the colorful Roscoe Turner and future World World War II hero Jimmy Doolittle, and some of the most innovative aeronautical engineering in the country, the races boosted Cleveland's aviation-related industry and thrilled hundreds of thousands of its citizens.

While sports may have signified status for some members of Cleveland's population, for many others games such as baseball and football and contests such as boxing and track and field became a means to prove one's self-worth and "Americanism," as well as avenues to a better life. Boxing was perhaps the first sport viewed by immigrants as the way to recognition and riches. However, it was not until the 1920s that boxing became a major part of the local sports picture.

This was largely because boxing matches not only had been frowned upon but

Fred Crawford presents the Thompson Trophy to Rudy Kling at the 1937 Cleveland National Air Races. The air races are credited with keeping up interest in aviation during the interwar era. *Western Reserve Historical Society.*

JOHN PATRICK "JOHNNY" KILBANE (18 Apr. 1889–31 May 1957), called Cleveland's "greatest champion," was the world featherweight boxing champion from 1912 to 1923. Trained by boxer Jimmy Dunn, Kilbane fought his first bout in Dec. 1907. By 1911 he was a contender on the boxing circuit in California. On 22 Feb. 1912, Kilbane defeated Abe Attell in a 20-round decision to win the featherweight crown, and was welcomed home to Cleveland on St. Patrick's Day by a crowd of 100,000. He ended his career 142–4, spending most of his later life in politics.

Johnny Kilbane smiles triumphantly in his corner after winning the decision for the featherweight championship of the world, 26 February 1912, in Los Angeles. *Cleveland Press Collection, Cleveland State University.*

actually had been illegal in Cleveland and Ohio during much of the preceding period. One of the first mentions of the activity in the city dates from 1855, when Professor Sheridan Mann offered classes in "the excellent ornamental and useful arts of sparring and fencing." In 1863 the *Cleveland Leader* reported on a match in the Flats between Paste Horne of England the James Hebard of Cleveland. In 1868 a state law made it illegal "for a person to be in any way connected with a fight or to countenance it by his presence." The matches that did take place were fought in neighboring states, on boats on Lake Erie, or within the private confines of clubs such as the Cleveland Athletic Club.

For a brief three-year period in the late 1890s, primarily during the mayoralty of "Honest" John Farley, boxing was again legal in Cleveland. During this time, on March 17, 1898, Clevelanders witnessed their first prizefight, a twenty-rounder at the Central Armory between Kid Lavigne and Jack Daly. Heroes of the ring, including John L. Sullivan and Bob Fitzsimmons, also sometimes appeared in Cleveland, albeit as part of vaudeville exhibitions. The ancestry of fighters such as Sullivan and Fitzsimmons made them models and champions for their respective ethnic groups. The Irish, in particular, saw the ring as a means to vindicate their national grievance against the English, as well as a way to achieve fame and status in the United States.

It was difficult, however, to cultivate the manly art in Cleveland, for the city's Progressive mayor, Tom L. Johnson, again banned fighting when he took office in 1901. Local gyms continued to train fighters, and to avoid legal interference fights were carefully staged outside the city limits at venues such as Casey's Woods on Berea Road. It was in this clandestine atmosphere that Cleveland's first true ethnic champion arose. John "Johnny" Patrick Kilbane grew up in the Irish west side neighborhood known as the Angle. Trained by Jimmy Dunn, he had his first fight in 1907, and in 1912 won the featherweight championship from Abe Attell in a match held in California. His triumphant return to Cleveland was heralded by the cheers of a crowd of 100,000 at the St. Patrick's Day parade. He was not only a city hero but a symbol of prowess and success to many in the Irish-American community.

Although Tom Johnson's successor, Herman Baehr, again legalized boxing in the city, the following mayor, reform-minded Newton D. Baker, banned the sport after he took office in 1912. His successor, Harry L. Davis, a street-smart politician like Baehr, again opened up the sport in the city and appointed Cleveland's first boxing commission to oversee the conduct of local bouts. In this manner he struck a compromise position by allowing a sport favored by "the people," but imposing civic regulation upon it to soothe the antiboxing faction. Local opinions of the sport

Jimmy Dunn, shown here with Johnny Kilbane prior to his championship bout in February 1912. *Cleveland Press Collection, Cleveland State University.*

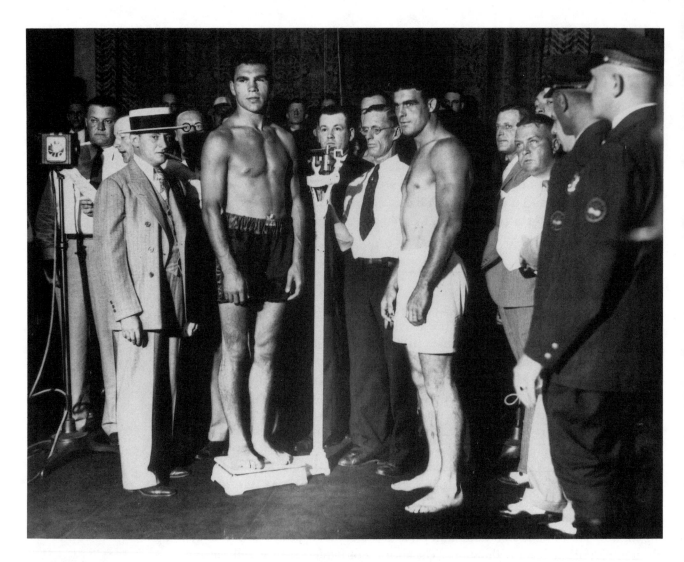

Germany's Max Schmeling and William "Young" Stribling weigh in for their heavyweight bout, 2 July 1931. *Cleveland Public Library.*

can be easily discerned in the actions of Cleveland's chief executives. Those who viewed themselves as reformers saw no redeeming value in the activity, while ward bosses, their allies, and the people were always ready to reinstitute boxing.

In any case, legalization of boxing would have had to occur during the 1920s and 1930s, because in those decades the sport achieved a national fame and legitimacy it had not previously enjoyed. The bouts of Jack Dempsey, Gene Tunney, Jack Sharkey, and Max Baer, among others, attracted enormous attention in the newspapers. Cleveland, though producing no major national champions of its own during

The SCHMELING-STRIBLING FIGHT on 3 July 1931 was the first heavyweight championship bout fought in Cleveland, as well as the first sporting event to be held at the recently completed Municipal Stadium. Schmeling, the German-born heavyweight champ, defeated "Willy the Whacker" Stribling, veteran of 300 pro boxing bouts, with a tenth-round technical knockout, virtually ending Stribling's quest for a title.

the 1920s and 1930s, did produce successful fighters who, like Kilbane, became symbols for their particular ethnic groups. Johnny Risko, of Slovak ancestry, became a nationally known heavyweight fighter, boxing with both Tunney and Baer—losing to the former and victorious over the latter. His chief attribute was that he was able to take a punch. Jackie Davis, "the Jewish Angel," fought 125 bouts between 1930 and 1935. His pride in his background was evidenced by the Star of David on his trunks.

Would-be community heroes were trained in local gyms such as Jack La Vack's

on Payne Avenue and East 19th Street, Charley Marotta's club on East 79th Street, and Mike Ryan's on Frankfort between West 6th and West 9th. In 1929 boxing received a tremendous boost with the beginning of the Golden Gloves amateur program in Cleveland. Suggested by Chicago sportswriter Arch Ward, Golden Gloves opened up boxing to youth across the country and assisted in its legitimation.

The acceptability of boxing in Cleveland was underscored when the first sporting event scheduled for the new Cleveland Municipal Stadium turned out to be a heavyweight championship fight. The contest between the champion, Max Schmeling of Germany, and William Stribling of Georgia (referred to in the press as Willy the Whacker) took place on July 3, 1931, and produced gate receipts of $349,000, an enormous sum for that Depression year. Schmeling won the fight and later went on to two fights which, though they had no direct connection to Cleveland, still had deep meaning for some of its citizens. These bouts with Joe Louis—Schmeling won the first and then was resoundingly defeated in the rematch—were milestones in the lives of Cleveland's African-American population. Louis, the nation's undefeated heavyweight champion throughout the 1930s, stood as a symbol for American blacks in Cleveland and other cities. Unlike the earlier black champion, Jack Johnson, Louis also gained a grudging acceptance from many whites. Touted by blacks and whites alike as a model for emulation, "a race man," Louis, through his many victories, set many local black youths on the road to boxing in the 1930s. The

Ted Green and the Case Institute football squad in 1903. At right halfback, Green led the team to an 8-1 record as Case outscored its opponents 245 to 53. *Case Western Reserve University Archives.*

MOSES FLEETWOOD "FLEET" WALKER (7 Oct. 1857–12 May 1924) was the first black baseball player in the major leagues. After playing college baseball at Oberlin and the University of Michigan, he joined the Toledo Blue Stockings, who won the championship of the Northwestern League in 1883. He remained with them in 1884 when the team joined the American Association, considered a major league at the time. Walker was a fine bare-handed catcher, but after an injury during the 1884 season he played sparingly and was released by Toledo in September. He played in the minor leagues through 1889, including a brief stay with a Cleveland team in the Western League.

Golden Gloves program opened many doors. A good number of black fighters from Cleveland owed their start to Louis's example and to the practical skills taught by Wilfred "Whiz Bang" Carter, a trainer active for many years on the near east side. Even future Cleveland mayor Carl Stokes tried his hand at boxing early in his life.

It wasn't easy for blacks to find hometown sporting heroes, however, as the segregation of professional and most amateur sports kept African-Americans out of the general limelight. It was a long time since Ted Green had been the football hero of the Case teams of 1902 and 1903 and the Reserve team of 1911. It was an even longer time since any black from northeastern Ohio had played baseball in the "big leagues." Moses Fleetwood Walker of Oberlin had played briefly for the Toledo team in the American Association during 1884, but then the open door in that

Moses Fleetwood Walker, shown here seated with the 1880 Oberlin College baseball team, was the first black to play in the major leagues. His brother Welday is in the rear. *Oberlin College Archives.*

league was shut, as were the doors in all other professional leagues. That is not to say there were no blacks in local professional baseball, because Cleveland fielded teams in the segregated Negro leagues throughout the 1920s and 1930s. These included the Cleveland Tate Stars of 1922, the Cleveland Browns of 1924, the Cleveland Elites of 1926, and the Cleveland Hornets of 1927. In 1931, the legendary Satchel Paige was a member of the Cleveland Cubs, a team which lasted for one brief season. Other teams, including the Cleveland Stars (1932), the Cleveland Giants (1933), the Cleveland Red Sox (1934), and the Cleveland Bears (1939–40), would come and go, their short lives evidence of the tenuous nature of their financing and the limited resources available for allocation to baseball in the Depression-stricken African-American community. Only the Buckeyes, a team which moved from Cincinnati to Cleveland in 1943, would last for any length of time. Their success would be part in the city's postwar sports history.

There was, however, one hometown black athlete who did achieve fame during the era of general sports segregation. In achieving that fame, Jesse Owens not only provided inspiration for local African Americans but made the name of the city internationally known. Born in Alabama, Owens came north to Cleveland with his family during the "great migration" from the American South to northern industrial cities. His track career was fostered by the programs in local schools, first at Fairmount Junior High, where he was coached by Charles Riley, and later at East Technical High School. After setting new local scholastic track records, he went on to college at Ohio State, where he continued to break records. His absolute triumph, however, was at the 1936 Berlin Olympics, where he won four gold medals—in the long jump, the 100 meters, the 200 meters, and the 400-meter relay. His triumphant return to Cleveland, celebrated in a parade, was cheered by all citizens, but the cheers were most heartfelt when his motorcade made its way through the city's Cedar Avenue black community.

Within Cleveland's white immigrant communities, American sports exerted a tremendous pull upon the younger generation. This is not to suggest that activities with Old World ties were completely abandoned during the 1920s and 1930s. On the contrary, some European sports which were to gain a general acceptance later in the century were widely played in these communities. One of these was association football, or soccer. A workingman's sport in Great Britain, and a popular activity on the Continent, it was brought to Cleveland during the 1920s and 1930s. The city had soccer clubs made up of Scots, English, Germans, Hungarians, and other nationalities. The game was so widespread in the local ethnic communities that at one time there were at least two Hungarian teams in the city. Hungarian immigrant Zoltan Gombos, who would go on to a career as a noted local newspaper publisher and patron of the arts, came to the city in the 1920s after having been a student soccer star in Hungary. He played here and got his start as a newspaper man by handling the sports pages for the local Hungarian paper (which he eventually bought), *Szabadsag*. On weekends during the 1920s, local soccer teams could be found vying against each other and out-of-town teams at Woodland Hills Park, which was located within the large Buckeye Hungarian community, at Luna Park or at private ethnic outing parks such as the German Central Farm on York Road in Parma.

In addition to fielding soccer teams, immigrants added new individual activities to the area's mix of sports. Lawn bowling was played by people of British extraction, while its counterparts, bocce, played by Italian-Americans, and bolinca, played by Slovenes, were found in the Murray Hill and St. Clair Avenue districts in which these groups resided. Indoor bowling, which had been brought to Cleveland by the

Germans, became widespread in the working-class community in the 1920s and 1930s.

German immigrants first introduced bowling—then a nine-pin game—to New York City in the 1840s. Later a tenth pin was added, supposedly to circumvent a New York City law that prohibited the game of nine-pins because of the gambling associated with it. In 1872 Cleveland saw its first bowling alley established on Bank (West 6th) Street. After 1900 the game began a rapid period of growth and acquired a clientele beyond the German community. The number of local alleys doubled dur-

Track legend Jesse Owens, running for Ohio State University, captures the hundred-yard dash in a record 9.4 seconds at a meet in Evanston, Ill., 18 May 1935. *Cleveland Press Collection, Cleveland State University.*

JESSE (JAMES CLEVELAND) OWENS (9 Sept. 1913–30 Mar. 1980) was a world-record-setting track-and-field athlete of the 1930s. Born on a tenant farm in Alabama, Owens came to Cleveland as a child. While attending Ohio State University, he broke or equaled 6 world records in one hour—in the 100-yard dash, long jump, 220-yard dash (also a record for the 200 meters), and 220-yard hurdles (also a record for the 200-meter hurdles)—at a meet in Ann Arbor, Mich., on 25 May 1935. Owens gained his greatest fame in the 1936 Berlin Olympics, where he won 4 gold medals and established new records in the 100- and 200-meter sprints, the 400-meter relay, and the long jump. In 1950, Owens was voted by sportswriters as the world's top track star of the century.

European sports played a prominent role in ethnic cohesion in Cleveland's many immigrant communities. In this instance, two soccer teams face off at Luna Park in April 1936. *Western Reserve Historical Society.*

ing the period 1901–1907. As the game grew, regulation became necessary. The American Bowling Congress had been established in St. Louis, one of the nation's most German cities, in 1895. Cleveland's affiliate of that body, the Cleveland Bowling Association, was created in 1905. In 1907 there were 29 leagues composed of 240 teams in the city. By 1937 there were 3,000 leagues with a membership of approximately 20,000 to 21,000. About one-third of the members were women.

Women's involvement in the sport began in the early part of the century. There was initial hesitancy regarding female participation because most alleys were working-class affairs attached to saloons where players could drink and gamble on

Area residents converge on Cedar Avenue for the parade celebrating Jesse Owens's victorious return from the 1936 Berlin Olympic Games, where he captured four gold medals. *Western Reserve Historical Society.*

STELLA WALSH (STANISLAWA WALASIEWICZ) (3 Apr. 1911–4 Dec. 1980) was a prominent female track star and was named in 1951 the "greatest female athlete of the first half of the 20th century." The Wierzchownen, Poland, native came to Cleveland as a child. At age 15 she tied the women's record for the 50-yard dash, and at the 1932 Los Angeles Olympics she won the 100-meter dash in world-record time while representing Poland. By 1946 Walsh held 65 world and national records. She was murdered during a robbery in 1980.

the outcome of the games. Some alleys, however, attempted to provide a more familylike atmosphere. By the 1910s, E. M. Helm's alleys on East 13th Street were recognized as a place where women could bowl. In 1916, the Women's National Bowling Congress was organized, and in 1918 Cleveland women created the Cleveland Women's Bowling Association to govern their participation in the game.

Polish Olympic heroine and Cleveland resident Stella Walsh throws the discus at the 1932 Los Angeles Olympic games, 4 August 1932. *Cleveland Press Collection, Cleveland State University.*

While bowling was an ethnic sport that gained converts from outside the German community, most immigrant groups saw their youth move away from sports such as soccer and into more traditionally "American" activities. The Sokol movement recognized this trend and added other sports to its gymnastic activities. The Sokol Polski, which served the city's Polish community, added basketball, baseball, boxing, and track to its programs in the 1920s. One of the youngsters who took advantage of the new offerings was Polish-born Stanislawa Walasiewicz, who would later gain fame as Stella Walsh. Walsh played baseball and basketball and participated in track-and-field events. Not then a naturalized citizen, she ran for the Polish team in the 1932 Olympic games, winning the 100-yard dash. By 1946 she held sixty-five world and national track-and-field records. As Jesse Owens was a symbol for the local black community, Walsh's achievements made her a source of great pride for the city's Poles.

While the Sokols may have taken up American sports in an attempt to keep ethnic youth interested in their programs, they did not all necessarily approve of the mercenary aspects of American sporting enterprise. In 1936 the local socialist Czech Workers Gymnastic Union sponsored a national "Workers Olympiad" in Cleveland as a counter to the international contests being staged in Nazi Germany, and as a protest against the capitalist control of sports within the United States. The event attracted hundreds of athletes from across the country.

The Workers Olympiad was, however, a protest headed by only a small portion of the city's diverse ethnic population. For many, particularly the children of immigrants, American sports were the best way to prove oneself—both as an athlete and as a member of a new society. Baseball, the city's oldest and most popular sport, provided the best proof.

In addition to being played on professional and amateur diamonds, baseball was a game of the city's immigrant neighborhoods. David Miller, writing in *Here in the Golden Land: A Vignette of Jewish Life in Cleveland,* noted that "the average child in the Woodland area [the principal Jewish immigrant neighborhood in the city in the early 1900s] received about one hour a day of Jewish instruction, force-fed by a harassed teacher. Jewish lore could not compete with baseball." Nor, for instance, could the Catholic church. Polish, Slovak, Czech, and other ethnic Catholic churches sponsored baseball teams for the youths of their parishes—it was one

The Workers Olympiad, held to protest both the Olympics being held in Nazi Germany and capitalist control of sports in the U.S., brought many athletes to Cleveland in 1936. *Western Reserve Historical Society.*

Young boys strain to get a peek at a ballgame in progress at League Park, ca. 1920. *Western Reserve Historical Society.*

of the only ways of keeping them close to the religious and cultural centers of their communities. Nationality newspapers, which numbered in the dozens in 1920s Cleveland, began running regular sports columns, just like the English-language dailies, in an attempt to hold on to a young readership.

Neither the priests and rabbis nor the newspaper editors of Cleveland's immigrant neighborhoods could ignore the pervasiveness of baseball. It was played in the schoolyard, in the street, and in empty lots throughout town. Young boys did not necessarily need a full set of equipment for a game. Stickball and handball versions

Cleveland native and Czech community hero Joe Vosmik bats for the Cleveland Indians, ca. 1935. A product of the sandlots, Vosmik batted over .300 for his career. *Western Reserve Historical Society.*

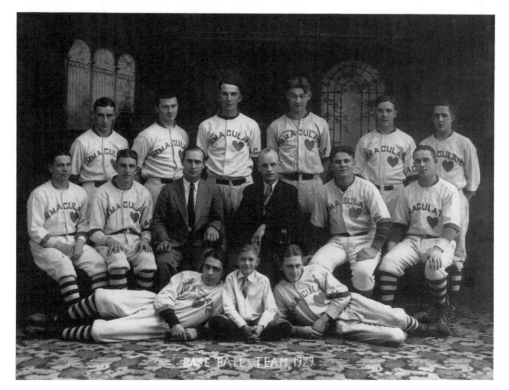

The Immaculate Heart of Mary baseball team in 1929. Ethnic churches around the city, such as this Polish Roman Catholic congregation, realizing the immense popularity of the game, sponsored baseball to attract young parishioners. *John Grabowski Collection.*

of baseball were common in Little Italy. Polish boys from the southeast side of Cleveland could keep balls in play well beyond their normal lifespans with a good application of friction tape. When a ball finally died, the boys would lie in the ravine behind the backstops at Washington Park waiting for a stray foul ball. When one came, they grabbed it and ran, their meager equipment replenished for a season. The heroes of the youth of the 1920s and 1930s throughout Cleveland and, in particular, in the working-class neighborhoods were, of course, baseball players named Speaker, Ruth, and Gehrig. But there was a special pride in the Czech community for Cleveland Indian outfielder Joe Vosmik, who had honed his skills on the Washington Park diamonds. Poles by the hundreds, including the members of the St. Stanislaus church band, turned up at League Park to watch future hall-of-famer Stanley Covelski pitch. His three victories in the 1920 World Series overshadowed any news from the recently reborn Polish homeland. Jews found a hero in Indians infielder Jonah Goldman. Italians in Cleveland had to look beyond the local professional team to "Push-em-up" Tony Lazzari of the Yankees, and later Joe DiMaggio. Local Slovenians took pride in Joe Kuhel, a product of the St. Clair neighborhood who played first base for the Chicago and Washington clubs. In finding their baseball heroes, the members of the city's newer immigrant groups repeated what the Irish and Germans had done before them in admiring the play of Michael "King" Kelley and Herman "Germany" Schaefer.

Many young men from Cleveland, both black and white, would eventually leave their insular neighborhoods when they joined or were drafted into the armed forces in World War II. They would carry their games with them to bases throughout the world and have the chance to test their skills against those of men from a variety of backgrounds. When those fortunate enough to return came back to Cleveland, they would be greatly changed by the experience of the war, as would their city. It would be wealthier, having finally escaped the Depression. The veterans themselves would have far different ideas about their place in the community and their rights as citizens. Those ideas would create a demand for job security, greater income and leisure time, and, for African-Americans, a demand that they no longer be treated as a separate league both in the workplace and on the playing field. The effect of these changed perceptions on sports in postwar Cleveland would be enormous. Whereas sports had been made an increasingly important social and economic part of the city in the years from 1918 to 1945, it would become the mirror of the city's social and economic fortunes in the coming decades.

Social Mirror, Economic Engine, and Civic Asset: Postwar Sports in Cleveland, 1946–1990

In his 1899 volume *The Theory of the Leisure Class,* Thorstein Veblen noted, "The addiction to sports, therefore, in a peculiar degree marks an arrested development of man's moral nature." Had Veblen visited Cleveland, indeed the United States, some ninety-one years after writing these lines, he would have believed he had stumbled upon a completely amoral society. Sports seemed both a local and a national addiction, and the "leisure class" had expanded beyond any limits Veblen could have imagined in the 1890s. In Cleveland he would have found a daily newspaper devoting at least one-fifth of its column space to sports, new electronic media devoting equal if not greater amounts of time to sports, and a chamber of commerce that no longer viewed sports as a civically valuable consequence of normal business enterprise but considered it a main supportive member of the local economy. More important, had he looked at the previous forty-five years of civic history in Cleveland, he would have noted a remarkable parallel between sports and civic progress—no longer an activity that seemed to take place independently of the city's development, sports became symbiotically linked to the social, political, and economic fortunes of post–World War II Cleveland. In most instances the changes in the city, and those in the nation which influenced the city, were transmitted to the arena. However, by the 1980s, the expected order of things had apparently reversed, as the economic dominance of sports had begun to influence the city's destiny.

Peaking Together:
Sports and Cleveland in the Late 1940s and 1950s

Immediately after World War II, winning teams and the racial integration of professional athletics coincided with urban growth and local civil rights activities to produce what some people might consider the greatest period in the city's history.

BILL VEECK (9 Feb. 1914–2 Jan. 1986) was the maverick owner of the Cleveland Indians from 1946 to 1949. After purchasing the franchise for $1,500,000 on 21 June 1946, the 32-year-old Chicago-born Veeck promoted the team through giveaways, fireworks, and strolling bands—anything to get the fans to the ballpark—and made Municipal Stadium the permanent home of the Indians. The club's attendance for 1948 was a record 2.6 million. In 1947 he signed Larry Doby, the first black in the American League, and he was instrumental in building the 1948 world championship team. Veeck went on to own the St. Louis Browns and the Chicago White Sox.

Cleveland had entered World War II as a former industrial giant just beginning to shake off the effects of the Depression. Its population had dropped during the 1930s, and despite New Deal reforms, many of its factories were still not working to capacity. The war changed all of that as plants were reopened, work forces expanded, and people flooded into the city. By 1946 the value of goods produced by industries in Cuyahoga County amounted to $2,673,300,000, more than 2.5 times the value of production in 1939. The labor force had increased by a factor of 1.6 during this time, and the industrial payroll had grown to 2.8 times its 1939 level. In 1950, the city would achieve its highest-ever population figure, 914,808.

Indians owner Bill Veeck, baseball's iconoclast chief executive, welcomes female fans to the first Indians "Ladies' Day" at the Stadium, July 1946. *Cleveland Press Collection, Cleveland State University.*

When servicemen and -women returned to Cleveland, they came back to a newly prosperous city as victors in the greatest conflict in history. The records of their professional sports teams would only serve to add to the general civic euphoria. Baseball, which was still by far the most popular area sport, provided the greatest thrill. In 1946, Bill Veeck, a thirty-two-year-old ex-Marine from Chicago, headed a syndicate that bought the Cleveland Indians franchise for $1,500,000. Veeck, who had worked for Bill Wrigley's Chicago Cubs, had his own ideas about how a baseball team should be run—ideas that were frowned upon by the conservative Wrigley. Veeck was a showman who thought the game should be an entertaining experience for the fans. He quickly added free orchids and nylons for the ladies, strolling bands, fireworks, and cheap beer to attract people to the Indians' games. The sideshows did draw fans, but more important, the strong Indians team, led by player-manager Lou Boudreau and supported by a stellar pitching staff featuring Bob Feller, played exciting and winning baseball. By 1947 Veeck's team was drawing so much attendance that all games had to be played in the Municipal Stadium, and the team's use of League Park ended. Attendance records continued to be shattered in 1948 as the Indians set major-league records for the largest crowds for a single game, doubleheader, night game, opening day game, and the season—a total of 2,620,627 saw them play that year. The regular season closed with a playoff game against the Boston Red Sox, which the Indians won, 8 to 3, thereby gaining the American League pennant. They then went on to defeat the National League Boston Braves, four games to two, in the World Series. For the first time in more than a quarter of a century, Cleveland had a world champion baseball team. Over 300,000 citizens lined a five-mile motorcade route to greet the team on their return to Cleveland from the sixth and final game in Boston. That crowd represented almost one-quarter of the people living in the Cleveland metropolitan area at that time.

Football also provided postwar Clevelanders with victories and championships. Following the departure of the 1945 NFL champion Rams for Los Angeles, a new team, the Cleveland Browns, became the city's professional football representatives, playing in the then one-year-old All-American Football Conference. The team was organized in April 1945 by Arthur B. "Mickey" McBride and Robert H. Gries. Gries, a well-to-do businessman and the son of one of the city's leading Reform rabbis, Moses H. Gries, had helped form the Rams in 1936. McBride, whose sometimes controversial career included real-estate ventures, newspapers and ownership of Cleveland's taxicab company, had never seen a football game until his son entered Notre Dame in 1940. His conversion to the sport was almost instantaneous. He would be one of the founders of the All-American Football Conference four years later. McBride's later use of Browns players on the reserve list as taxi drivers led to the use of the terms "cab" or "taxi" squad for reserve players.

This unlikely pair, a no-holds-barred Irish-American businessman and the well-educated scion of one of the city's oldest Jewish families, united to produce what would become one of the most successful and profitable professional sports franchises in the city and the nation. A large measure of their success was due to their choice of head coach, Paul Brown, after whom the team was named. Brown came to the team after a career coaching high-school and college football. Immediately before joining the Cleveland franchise, he had been coach of the Ohio State team. Brown's emphasis on intelligence, speed, and character in his players, along with his good fortune in being able to select talent from the pool of former college players now available after completing their military service, almost guaranteed the success of the franchise.

The team, which included stars such as quarterback Otto Graham, Lou Groza, Dante Lavelli, Marion Motley, and Bill Willis, went on to win the AAFC championship each year from 1946 to 1949. In 1950 the Browns shifted to the National Football League. Few thought they would do as well in the older and "tougher" circuit. Surprising the doubters, they won the championship, defeating the Los Angeles Rams for the title. Despite this victorious record, it was still difficult for the team to earn its way, given the short football season and the rather small turnouts at each game (average pro football game attendance in 1950 was only 25,000). Robert D. Gries, who succeeded his father in partial ownership of the team, recalls instances in the 1940s when the team owners would sit down with the laundry bills and other invoices and decide just how the bills and players' salaries were going to be met out of the day's gate receipts.

Clevelanders even had a winning team in ice hockey. During the late 1940s, the Cleveland Barons dominated the American Hockey League championship. The Calder Cup trophy resided in the city in 1944, 1945, 1947, 1948, 1950, and 1951. Playing in the largest metropolitan region in minor-league hockey, Al Sutphin's team regularly attracted 10,000 people to the Arena.

One other major Cleveland team would win championships in the late 1940s.

Player-manager Lou Boudreau waits on deck to bat during the 1948 season. *Cleveland Press Collection, Cleveland State University.*

BACK AGAIN in '48 to give you THE BEST SHOW IN FOOTBALL

Edgar Jones, HB

Marion Motley, FB

Lou Saban, FB

Otto Graham, QB

Dante Lavelli, E

Lou Rymkus, T

Bill Willis, G

Frank Gatski, C

Ed Ulinski, G

Lou Groza, T

Mac Speedie, E

Paul Brown, Coach

7 TICKETS FOR THE PRICE OF SIX!

3.60 SEAT **21.60 PER BOOK**

2.40 SEAT **14.40 PER BOOK**

I WAS CLEAN SHAVEN AT THE END OF THE LINE!

NO WAITING!

Your purchase of a SEASON TICKET now not only saves you money but eliminates waiting in line later on. Your SEASON TICKET guarantees you the same choice seat for each of the Cleveland Browns' seven home games

TICKETS

How To Order:

Fill out TICKET APPLICATION on reverse side of folder. Please print clearly. Mail application and remittance to
　Ticket Manager
　Cleveland Browns
　405 Leader Building
　Cleveland 14, Ohio
Orders will be filled based on date of receipt Season ticket sale closes Saturday, Aug. 21 For further information, phone TOwer 1-0874

This Browns season ticket promotional brochure delivered on its promise to provide "the best show in football." The Browns won all four All-American Football Conference championships from 1946 to 1949. *Western Reserve Historical Society.*

The Cleveland Buckeyes won the Negro American League pennant in 1945 and 1947. Led by centerfielder Sam Jethro, the Buckeyes went on in 1945 to defeat the Homestead Grays in the Negro World Series. In 1947 the team lost the series one game to four to the New York Cubans. Playing their home games at League Park, the Buckeyes fielded and hosted some of the best black baseball talent in the country, including Jethro, Satchel Paige, Josh Gibson, and "Cool Papa" Bell. For black Clevelanders, the Buckeyes were a source of both pride and disappointment. The team was a winner, but its very existence was a reminder of the disparities between blacks and whites both in sports and in American society. However, while the Buckeyes were compiling their postwar winning record, changes occurred that would lead to greater equality on the playing field.

By 1950, the number of African-Americans in Cleveland had risen to 147,850, nearly 16 percent of the city's population. Fleeing segregation and poverty in the American South, African Americans would dominate the movement of new people to the city in the years to come. With immigration from Europe largely curtailed by quota restrictions, the percentage of blacks in the city's population would continue to rise throughout the 1950s and 1960s. The changes did not go unrecognized by the city's leadership.

While in the pre–World War II period the city had largely ignored its growing black population and the discrimination that confronted local African-Americans in

ARTHUR B. "MICKEY" McBRIDE (20 Mar. 1888–10 Nov. 1972), a local businessman, founded the Cleveland Browns professional football team in 1944, and helped organize the 8-team All-American Football Conference (AAFC), in which the Browns played from 1946 to 1949. After hiring Paul Brown as head coach, he used his promotional skills to build fan support for the club, including a contest to name the team. In spite of McBride's financial help to other league owners, the AAFC collapsed in 1949, and he arranged for the Browns to join the National Football League. In 1953 he sold the team to a group of Cleveland businessmen for about $600,000.

housing, employment and sports, at the end of that conflict Cleveland became one of the nation's most forward-looking cities in matters of race relations. Spurred in part by worsening local conditions and by the very nature of World War II—a conflict fought against the racist Nazi German regime—Cleveland's city government realized that the situation would have to change. With the formation in 1945 of the nation's first municipal community relations board and passage of fair employment legislation in 1950, Cleveland tried to mitigate the most obvious effects of racial prejudice. It would be safe to say that through such actions the city took a position of national leadership in the area of race relations.

Clevleland Browns founder Arthur McBride signs over controlling interest of the team to Dave Jones, the new owners' representative, 10 June 1953. *Cleveland Public Library.*

Cleveland Browns organizer Robert H. Gries in 1931. Gries's family still retained partial ownership interest in the Browns nearly five decades after the team's inception in 1946. *Cleveland Press Collection, Cleveland State University.*

This attitude was almost immediately reflected within local professional sports. While Branch Rickey was the first to break the color barrier in the National League by signing Jackie Robinson to his Brooklyn Dodger organization in 1946, Bill Veeck signed outfielder Larry Doby, the first black to play in the American League, in 1947. In 1948, Veeck would bring the ageless pitcher Satchel Paige, one of the all-time Negro League greats, to the Indians. The Cleveland Browns, under the leadership of Paul Brown, broke the football color barrier in the All-American Conference in 1946 when they signed Marion Motley and Bill Willis to the team. Interestingly enough, the Rams of Los Angeles, a former Cleveland team, were the first to sign black players (Woody Strode and Kenny Washington) in the National Football League. Life for pioneering black professional athletes was anything but easy. In addition to enduring the taunts from opposing teams, players such as Willis and Motley found they had no roommates except each other while on the road. Being on the road in segregated cities could provide additional problems when the black members of a team were refused the same services offered to their white teammates.

The entry of blacks into formerly whites-only professional sports had other consequences as well. For better or worse, skimming the cream of the best talent of the Negro baseball leagues left the teams in those leagues in a noncompetitive

Legendary Browns coach
Paul Brown kneels on the
sidelines surrounded by
star players Otto Graham
(*in helmet*), Dante Lavelli,
and Lou Groza (*standing*),
during a December 1951
game. *Cleveland Press
Collection, Cleveland
State University.*

position vis-à-vis formerly all-white professional teams. One by one, the teams
folded, and the Negro leagues had collapsed entirely by 1960. The Cleveland Buckeyes, for example, broke up after a poor 1948 season. An attempted comeback in
1950 ended after half the season, with the team winning only three of its first thirty-
six games. During the early years of baseball's integration, when only a small number of blacks were added to the major-league teams, many black ballplayers of
average to slightly better than average talent had only the Negro leagues in which to
play. Their career hopes usually ended when those leagues folded. Despite such
consequences, the integration of professional sports came none too soon. Clevelanders could take pride in breaking down some racial barriers, both within the city
and on their sports teams.

While black athletes such as Motley, Willis, and Doby helped the area's professional teams to victory, Harrison Dillard, an African-American graduate of East

OTTO GRAHAM (6 Dec. 1921–   ) played quarterback for the Cleveland Browns from 1946 to 1955. Although he had been a tailback at Northwestern University, as quarterback "Automatic" Graham was selected to the all-AAFC (All-America Football Conference) team each year from 1946 to 1949; additionally, he was named to the NFL Pro Bowl in 1951–53 and 1955. On 14 Oct. 1949, Graham threw 6 touchdown passes against the Los Angeles Dons, and in 1953 he had a 64.7 pass completion percentage. Graham compiled 174 career touchdown passes and was elected to the Pro Football Hall of Fame in 1965.

Technical High School and Baldwin Wallace College, once again put the city in the international spotlight through his Olympic performances. Dillard duplicated Jesse Owens's victory in the 100-meter sprint during the London games of 1948, and four years later won the gold medal in the 110-meter hurdles at the Helsinki games. Sixteen years later another African-American from Cleveland, Madeline Manning, would gain international recognition for the city by winning the 800-meter race at the Mexico City Olympics.

Cleveland sports fans had much to look forward to when the 1950s began. Not only were local teams winning, but citizens had more time and money than ever

Browns quarterback Otto Graham "discusses" the game with #56 Dante Lavelli after the Browns defeated the New York Yankees to win the first AAFC championship at Municipal Stadium, 22 December 1946. *Cleveland Press Collection, Cleveland State University.*

Otto Graham goes end-around for an eighteen-yard gain against the San Francisco 49ers at Cleveland Municipal Stadium before being injured on the tackle, 17 November 1953. *Cleveland Press Collection, Cleveland State University.*

before to enjoy sports. Blue-collar workers moved into the middle-income class as labor unions, legitimized during the New Deal, won higher wages for their members, as well as a standard five-day week of eight-hour workdays. Some Clevelanders who had served in World War II used the GI Bill to obtain college educations and move beyond the factory floor. All in all, people had more money to spend and a plethora of ways in which to spend it. Most chose automobiles and what would become the ultimate sports machine, the television. Nothing did more than TV to change the nature of sports in the United States and Cleveland.

The local media—first newspapers, then radio, and finally television—had served to popularize sports since the 1890s. It was during that decade that Cleveland newspapers, particularly the *Cleveland Press* and the *Cleveland World*, which catered to the tastes of the common man, began to devote significant space in each issue to sports, thereby creating the sports page. All local newspapers were giving great attention to sports by the early 1900s, and by the 1920s sportswriting was a major facet of local journalism. Eventually the city produced such noted sportswriters as Ed Bang and Ed McCauley of the *Cleveland News*, Gordon Cobbledick of the *Plain Dealer*, and Franklin Lewis of the *Cleveland Press*. While newspapers could describe what had happened in the previous day's contests, radio could not only give results but also provide live coverage of the games. Radio began in Cleveland in 1922 when WHK became the city's first station. That station began broadcasts of Cleveland Indians games in 1931. Over the following years Cleveland listeners would follow games described by noted announcers Tom Manning, Jack Graney, Jimmy Dudley, and Bob Neal. By 1936 WHK was broadcasting the full Indians season.

LOU "THE TOE" GROZA (25 Jan. 1924–) played tackle and place-kicked for the Cleveland Browns from 1946 to 1967, missing only the 1960 season because of an injury, and was the last of the "original" Browns to retire. Groza, an Ohio State alumnus, competed in 4 All-America Football Conference and 9 National Football League title games; he kicked the winning field goal for the Browns in the 1950 championship. He was limited to kicking after 1960. Groza scored 1,608 points in 21 years as a pro and played in 9 Pro Bowls. He was inducted into the Pro Football Hall of Fame in 1974.

Six-time All-Pro Lou "The Toe" Groza watches one of his kicks sail toward the goalposts in a game with the St. Louis Cardinals in October 1967. *Cleveland Press Collection, Cleveland State University.*

DANTE "GLUE FINGERS" LAVELLI (23 Feb. 1923–   ) was a member of the first Cleveland Browns football team in 1946 and played 10 seasons with them. He was an outstanding pass receiver; his ability to catch the football was recognized in both the All-American Conference and the National Football League, where he was named all-pro end a total of 8 times. He was inducted into the Professional Football Hall of Fame in 1975.

Hearing a sporting event described live on radio was, of course, a great improvement over reading about that event one day later. Seeing it live on television was even better. Cleveland's first station, WEWS, began broadcasting in 1947. By 1949 the city had three stations on the air. In May of that year WEWS aired its first live broadcast of a Cleveland Indians game. By the 1950s Clevelanders could regularly relax in their own homes while watching baseball, played by the Indians or other teams, as well as college and professional football, boxing, wrestling, and a variety of other sports.

The consequences of sports broadcasts on television were enormous. TV contracts provided franchises with additional funds. As team income increased, so did salary demands and interest on the part of more entrepreneurs to found new leagues

Browns running back Dante Lavelli bursts through a hole in the Buffalo Bisons' defensive line for a big gain during the Browns' inaugural season in 1946. *Cleveland Press Collection, Cleveland State University.*

FRANK "GUNNER" GATSKI (13 Mar. 1922–   ) was a member of the first Cleveland Browns football team in 1946 and played 11 seasons with them. At center, Gatski had both the size and the strength to be equally effective as a pass protector or as a blocker on running plays. His skills were recognized when he was elected to the Professional Football Hall of Fame in 1985.

and even sports in order to get in on the money-making opportunity. Of course, a televised home game could cut revenues at the park. Seeing this potential problem, Dan Reeves, owner of the Los Angeles Rams football team, began employing local blackouts of Rams games. In 1953, when blackouts were challenged in the courts as a restraint of trade, a federal judge ruled in favor of the practice, and the golden era of TV sports was on. The $200,000 spent by team owners to plead their case turned out to be well spent.

While professional teams benefited from television, portions of the amateur world suffered. The fact that big-league action could be viewed in virtually any home in the United States caused the number of minor-league ball teams to shrink from over 450 in the 1940s to a mere 171 in 1991. In Cleveland, the crowds at the sandlot diamonds diminished as big-league ball became accessible in the living

Cleveland Browns center Frank Gatski (#52) with Lou Groza in 1956. *Cleveland Press Collection, Cleveland State University.*

MIKE McCORMACK (21 June 1930–) was an offensive tackle for the New York Yankees in his rookie year and for the Cleveland Browns from 1954 to 1963. Adept at protecting the quarterback and opening holes for the running back, McCormack earned a place in the Pro Bowl 6 times during his 10-year career. His skills were recognized when he was inducted into the Professional Football Hall of Fame in 1984. After his retirement as a player, McCormack coached in the National Football League.

room. As television executives decided to focus their college football coverage on major teams such as those in the Big Ten, small schools such as Reserve, Case, Baldwin Wallace, and John Carroll saw their games attended only by students, friends, and alumni. Since the big schools needed to recruit better and better talent to look good in front of larger audiences, they lobbied for and received permission from the NCAA to grant full athletic scholarships in 1952. Unable and unwilling to compete in this type of market, Cleveland's colleges pulled away completely from big-time football. In 1954 they organized the Presidents' Athletic Conference, which banned athletic scholarships and attempted to foster a less expensive regional competition.

Perhaps the greatest consequence of television was the tremendous boost in popularity it gave to professional football. By the mid-1960s the Cleveland Browns could justly claim to be the city's most popular sports team—the one-hundred-year reign of baseball as king of local sports seemed to be over. Football was a sports custom made for the new electronic medium. It had lots of action, but that action was sporadic, allowing a significant amount of time to be devoted to commentary

Browns lineman Mike McCormack (#74) roll-blocks for running back Fred Morrison (#32), leading to a 12-yard gain against the Washington Redskins, 9 November 1954. *Cleveland Press Collection, Cleveland State University.*

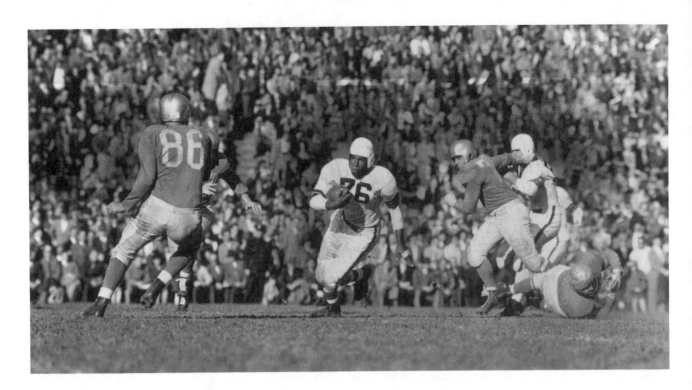

Marion Motley (#76) runs into the open field for the Browns in November 1947. *Cleveland Press Collection, Cleveland State University.*

and advertisements. Given huddles and sets and the short duration of most plays, it was not unusual for actual playing time to take up less than a quarter of the one-hour game. With time-outs and other breaks, the duration of a game usually stretched beyond two hours. And since football was a cold-weather sport, television could accommodate those interested in the game but not hardy enough to brave the stands in November or December. The potential of television revenues and the extraordinary record of the Browns made the team one of sports' most valuable commodities. In 1953 Mickey McBride sold his interest in the team for $600,000, half going to Saul Silberman and the remainder to a syndicate of businessmen headed by Dave R. Jones, a local industrialist. Just two years later, Silberman was able to sell his portion to the syndicate for $1.3 million. Only six years after that, former New York advertising executive Arthur B. Modell purchased a majority share in the team for $3,925,000. Modell's purchase of the Browns came three years

MARION MOTLEY (5 June 1920–   ), one of the first African-Americans in professional football, was a member of the Cleveland Browns under coach Paul Brown from 1946 to 1953. Out of South Carolina State College, Motley (#76) was a "60-minute man," playing linebacker and fullback for the Browns. In his career, he compiled 4,720 yards rushing, 1,107 yards receiving, 38 touchdowns, and 1,122 yards returning kickoffs, with an exceptional 23.4-yard average. Motley was elected to the Pro Football Hall of Fame in 1968.

Centerfielder Sam "The Jet" Jethroe of the Negro National League Cleveland Buckeyes, the 1945 Negro League World Champions. *Cleveland Press Collection, Cleveland State University.*

The CLEVELAND BUCKEYES were the last of many Cleveland teams which played in the Negro baseball leagues. Organized by Ernest Wright and Wilbur Hayes, the Buckeyes began play in 1943 with many former members of the Cincinnati Buckeyes, including such notable Negro All-Stars as Sam "the Jet" Jethro and player/manager Quincy Trouppe. The team, playing in the Negro American League with games held at League Park, made two appearances in the Negro World Series, sweeping the Homestead Grays in 1945, and losing to the New York Cubans in 1947. The Buckeyes folded after the 1948 season.

after what may have been the most important televised football game in history, the 1958 playoff between the Baltimore Colts and the New York Giants. An estimated viewing audience of 45 million watched as the evenly matched teams battled to a last-minute tie, and then saw the Colts win in sudden-death overtime. This exciting contest whetted the public's appetite for the game. Within twelve years, televised football would capture American viewing audiences.

Modell had purchased a winning team in a winning sport. After their championship debut in the NFL, the Browns, with Otto Graham as quarterback, won back-to-back championships in 1954 and 1955. With the retirement of many of the team's initial stalwarts in 1956, the Browns suffered their first losing season. The selection of Jim Brown of Syracuse University in the eighth round of the following year's draft would ensure them a winning record during his entire tenure (1957–1965) with the team, as he went on to become one of the game's greatest running backs.

Growing interest in the professional game served to spur amateur football in Cleveland. The number of teams sponsored by the Catholic Youth Organization (founded in late 1937) and the Muny Football Association increased significantly. High-school football, in particular, rose to new heights of popularity as school players now not only could emulate the pros but could hope for full athletic scholarships to college and, perhaps, for a professional career beyond that. During the 1950s and 1960s, play in the East and West athletic senates attracted considerable local attention. Play in the senate leagues was dominated by the parochial high schools, St. Ignatius, Cathedral Latin, Benedictine, and, to a somewhat lesser degree,

Hall of Fame defensive tackle Bill Willis at the Browns' training camp in 1951. *Cleveland Press Collection, Cleveland State University.*

LAWRENCE "LARRY" DOBY (23 Dec. 1923–) played outfield with the Cleveland Indians from 1947 to 1955 and again in 1958. Doby, a standout with the Newark Eagles of the Negro League, was signed by Indians owner Bill Veeck and became the first black to play in the American League, making his debut 5 July 1947. Doby played in 2 World Series (1948 and 1954) and 6 consecutive All-Star games. He finished his career with a .286 average, 215 home runs, and 969 runs batted in, and went on to become a coach and then a manager (with the 1978 Chicago White Sox) at the major-league level.

Holy Name. Jealous backers of the public high schools continually remonstrated that the student population of the parochial schools was recruited citywide, while their student bodies were drawn from smaller districts. Within the senate leagues, traditional school rivalries cropped up. That between South High and its Broadway Avenue neighbor, Holy Name, was of particular interest. The trophy over which the two schools battled was a slab of pig iron mounted on a board—it symbolized the jobs the grandparents and great-grandparents of the boys (largely Polish from South High and Irish from Holy Name) had battled over during strikes in the area's steel plants some seventy years before. Although large-scale immigration to the city had ceased in the early 1920s, ethnic rivalries remained an important facet of local sports when teams still represented neighborhoods in which one nationality or racial group predominated.

The only local scholastic sport that could rival the popularity of football in the 1950s was basketball. On the college level, Cleveland schools such as Case, Western Reserve, and John Carroll stayed away from big-time play, as they did in football,

(LEFT) **Indians centerfielder Larry Doby chats with Joe DiMaggio at spring training in 1951.** *Cleveland Press Collection, Cleveland State University.*

(RIGHT) **Bill Veeck watches pitching immortal Leroy "Satchel" Paige warm up in 1948.** *Cleveland Press Collection, Cleveland State University.*

HARRISON "BONES" DILLARD (8 July 1923–   ) was the first man in Olympic history to win gold medals in both the 100-meter dash (1948) and the 110-meter hurdles (1952). He was awarded 2 more gold medals as a member of the winning 100-meter relay team in 1948 and 1952. A state hurdles champion at Cleveland East Tech High, he later set world records in the 120-yard high and 220-yard low hurdles at Baldwin-Wallace College and once held 11 world, Olympic, and American records simultaneously. Dillard was voted the Sullivan Award in 1955 as the nation's outstanding amateur athlete.

through their participation in the Presidents' Athletic Conference. The PAC helped to mitigate possible corruption within local collegiate basketball. At the time of its creation, big-time collegiate basketball carried a particular onus because of the point-shaving scandals of 1951, when thirty-three players were accused of manipulating the point spread in order to get money from professional gamblers. The NCAA's decision to allow full athletic scholarships, which supposedly eliminated the players' needs for money, was its way of combating the evil. The Cleveland collegiate response was to avoid the big-game syndrome and to concentrate on academics and keep athletics ancillary. High-school basketball in Cleveland was

Baldwin-Wallace star and future Olympian Harrison Dillard sets a new world record of 7.1 seconds for the 60-yard indoor hurdles at the Chicago Relays, 21 March 1948. *Cleveland Public Library.*

much more noteworthy than the collegiate game during the decade, thanks largely to the spectacular play of the East Technical High School team. The Scarabs won three state and dozens of senate, city, sectional, district, and regional basketball championships in the 1950s. The teams from East Tech, which was located in the city's major black neighborhood, reflected the growing skill in the sport of inner-city youth and stood as a symbol of pride for the African-American community. The dominance of East Tech and Cleveland in high-school basketball was such that the state finals were held at the Cleveland Arena in 1954 and 1956.

While crowds filled the Arena for high-school basketball and at least two AAU college championship matches, postwar entrepreneurs could not hit upon a formula that would allow professional basketball to prosper in Cleveland. Perhaps the amateur game was just too strong to be challenged. Just before, during, and after the war, the city fielded four teams in the National Basketball League. Three of these, the Cleveland White Horses of 1938–39, the Chase Brass and Copper team of 1943, and the Allman Transfers of 1944–45, were former industrial league teams which, despite excellent players such as Mel Reibe, were unable to last more than two seasons. In 1946, Arena owner Al Sutphin organized the Cleveland Rebels to play in the new Basketball Association of America. The opening-night crowd of 7,594 on November 3, 1946, seemed to bode well for the success of the franchise, but by early 1947 crowds had dwindled. After compiling a 30 and 30 record for the season, the Rebels disbanded. At the beginning of the next decade, investors made yet another attempt to establish professional basketball in Cleveland. This time George Steinbrenner, local industrialist and future owner of the New York Yankees, entered his Cleveland Pipers in the new American Basketball League. The Pipers, formerly champions of the amateur industrial league in 1960–61, lasted only one year. Directed by John McLendon, the first black coach in professional basketball, the Pipers struggled to attract people to their games. Coscheduling Pipers games with exhibitions featuring the Harlem Globetrotters or a team composed of Cleveland Browns football players did little to improve the situation. A last-ditch effort to salvage the team by signing Ohio State Star Jerry Lucas failed when the team was financially unable to take to the court in 1962. The league also collapsed later that year.

Although the professional sports loyalties of many Americans and Clevelanders were being won over by football, baseball remained popular in the 1950s. New stars including Mickey Mantle and Willie Mays arose to capture the imaginations of the nation's youth. In Cleveland, for at least a while, it seemed as if the Indians would continue their winning tradition of the late 1940s. Bill Veeck maintained his ownership of the Indians through 1949, but then, because of financial difficulties, he sold the team to a syndicate headed by Ellis Ryan and former Detroit Tiger slugger Hank Greenberg. The sale price of $2.2 million represented a profit of $700,000 for Veeck, who had acquired the franchise only three years before. With the outstanding pitching staff of Bob Feller, Bob Lemon, Early Wynn, and Mike Garcia, the team continued to play extraordinary baseball, but it always found itself just behind the New York Yankees. In second place each season from 1949 through 1953, the Indians finally came out on top in 1954, winning a record 111 games. Their defeat of the Yankees for that year's pennant took place in front of an all-time record crowd of 84,587 at a September 12 doubleheader. That victory was perhaps the apogee of the team's history. The slide from the peak began with the World Series, which the Indians lost in four straight games to the New York Giants. The destiny of the team was summed up in the most memorable play of that Series, the

1968 Olympic 800-meter champion Madeline Manning, shown here in July of 1969, ran for three U.S. Olympic teams (1968, 1972, 1976) and topped the World Rankings for three years in a row, 1967 to 1969. *Cleveland Plain Dealer.*

Plain Dealer **sportswriter Gordon Cobbledick "pounds the keyboard" in the pressbox at Municipal Stadium, ca. 1955.** *Cleveland Press Collection, Cleveland State University.*

spectacular catch made by Willie Mays of a 450-foot drive off the bat of Indian Vic Wertz. No effort, no matter how large, could help the Indians thereafter; the fates seemed to be against them and, indeed, the city.

During the remainder of the decade, the team would slip from its preeminent position, as would attendance figures. Even the pennant-winning club of 1954 attracted nearly a million fewer fans than did the 1948 team. By 1959 attendance dropped below the one million mark for the first time since the Bill Veeck era. Contemporaneously, the entire foundation of major-league baseball began to destabilize as once-solid franchises were moved from city to city in search of bigger crowds and more income. In 1953 the Boston Braves moved to Milwaukee; in 1954 the St. Louis Browns became the Orioles of Baltimore; and in 1955 the Philadelphia Athletics took up residence in Kansas City. Most disconcerting of all to baseball purists were the moves in 1958 of the Brooklyn Dodgers and New York Giants to Los Angeles and San Francisco, respectively. Nothing was sacred anymore. The next owners of the Indians, Cleveland businessmen William R. Daley and Ignatius A. O'Shaughnessy, had paid $3.96 million for the franchise in 1956 and were obviously concerned about turning a profit. The team's play and fan attendance were not encouraging. Fate continued to damn all efforts. In 1958, the Indians' most promising new pitcher in years, Herb Score, was struck in the eye by a line drive off the bat

EDWARD F. "ED" BANG (28 Apr. 1880–27 Apr. 1968) was the sports editor for the *Cleveland News* for 53 years of its 55-year existence. The Sandusky, Ohio, native become sports editor of the *News* in 1907, and also helped to found the Baseball Writers' Association of America, in addition to aiding in the organization of the Cleveland Baseball Federation. In 1916, Bang played a key role in the Indians' acquisition of Tris Speaker. Bang's column promoted such sporting events in Cleveland as the 1931 Schmeling-Stribling fight. Bang retired in 1960 after the *News* was purchased by the Cleveland *Press*.

of Yankee Gil McDougald. Score would later return briefly to the mound, but the early promise of his career would never be fulfilled. As attendance continued to lag that year, rumors about a possible move of the team began to spread.

The response to the possibility of the team's leaving Cleveland came from a broadly representative spectrum of the community—loyal fans, local government, and the Chamber of Commerce. Baseball was by now too much a part of the civic ego and economic system to be lost without a fight. A "Back the Indians" program supported by City Council president Jack Russell and Lee Howley of the Chamber of Commerce drummed up larger crowds for the games and staved off the move. The business leadership of Cleveland now realized that the team was not merely a civic asset but a multimillion-dollar asset integral to the local economy. Seemingly in response to the community's expression of concern and interest, the Indians rebounded in 1959, finishing in second place. The achievement was due in part to the team's latest star and the city's newest sports hero, Italian-American Rocky

(LEFT) **Former** *Cleveland News* **sportswriter Ed Bang poses with I. S. "Nig" Rose (***left***), February 1964.** *Cleveland Press Collection, Cleveland State University.*

(RIGHT) **Indians broadcast team Jack Graney (***left***) and Jimmy dudley converse after an Indians game, 10 May 1948.** *Cleveland Press Collection, Cleveland State University.*

Colavito. Colavito hit forty-one home runs in 1958 and forty-two in the 1959 season. His popularity was such that children all over town performed their on-deck warmups just like "The Rock" by placing their upper arms behind a bat stretched across their backs. When in April 1960 the team's general manager, Frank Lane, announced the trade of Colavito to the Detroit Tigers, citizens were outraged. In trading The Rock, as well as a number of other players, Lane undermined fan loyalty and crushed the short-lived Cleveland Indians renaissance. For the next two decades the city's baseball team, as well as other of its sports activities, would spiral downward in the general confusion and despair that characterized the city's history from the 1960s to the 1980s.

Two Decades of Decline, 1960–1980

Tom Manning (*center, holding microphone*) participates in a pre-game broadcast at Municipal Stadium with local radio personalities Glen Rowell and Gene Carroll, ca. **1932.** *Cleveland Public Library.*

If Clevelanders had observed events carefully during 1960, they might have perceived the direction their city would take in the coming years. The city's population had slipped to 876,050, and factories were beginning to leave outmoded sites in the city for new nonunion locations in the American South. The descendants of the immigrants were also leaving the city, moving in large numbers to suburbs: Parma, Lyndhurst, Fairview Park, and South Euclid. While they left, new people came to the city in the full belief that it would fulfill their dreams just as it had those of earlier migrants. Increasing numbers of African-Americans, Appalachians, and Puerto Ricans arrived, looking for good jobs in an industrial sector that was melting away before them. These trends, begun in the 1950s, accelerated during the 1960s and 1970s. By 1980, the city's population decreased to 573,822. Riots, a burning river, fiscal default, and a collapsing school system were the legacies of these two decades, during which the story of local sports seemed equally sorry and just as fractious as relations between local politicians, neighborhoods, and the city and its suburbs.

Nothing characterized the dismal decline of the city so much as the fortunes of its baseball team. The record of the Indians barely approached mediocrity during these twenty years. A third-place finish in 1968 marked their high point. They played above .500 only twice in the 1970s. In 1964 they finished in fifth place, and in 1969 they fell to last place. That year they attracted only 619,970 fans to the sta-

LEONARD "LEN" FORD (18 Feb. 1926–14 Mar. 1972) was a star defensive end for the Cleveland Browns pro football team from 1950 to 1957. An All-American at Michigan in 1946 and 1947, he played two years with the Los Angeles Dons of the All-America Football Conference before coming to Cleveland. An outstanding pass rusher, Ford was named to the NFL All-Star team each year from 1951 to 1955. He was elected to the Pro Football Hall of Fame in 1976.

dium. Throughout the period, the team was sold and resold. In 1962, a nineteen-man local syndicate that included Vernon Stouffer, Thomas Burke, Frank J. O'Neill, and Gabe Paul bought the franchise from the Daley group for $6 million. Ten years later another group of local businessmen headed by sports entrepreneur Nick Mileti paid $9.7 million to acquire the team. They held the franchise for only six years before the O'Neill family, led by Francis J. O'Neill, gained control.

Throughout this period the team was constantly rumored to be on the verge of leaving the city. Such talk surfaced in 1964 when the Indians dropped to fifth place. In 1972 owners discussed the possibility of having the Indians play some of their games in New Orleans. Such an action would have had a parallel in the 1890s Spiders, who had been dubbed the Wanderers because of the multiple sites for their "home" games. It was not that the ownership was unimaginative in trying to coax people to the ballpark during these troubled times. There were bat days and ball days when free bats and balls were given to children attending the game. And there was "Beer Night." This event in 1974 featured ten-cent glasses of beer, producing a crowd so rowdy that the Indians were forced to forfeit the game. It was not free bats and balls or cheap beer that the fans wanted; it was a winning ball team. As the Indians' farm system fell apart and its roster changed on an almost daily basis, and as the cost of first-rate players skyrocketed, the goal of putting together a winning team seemed impossible. With poor gate income, the team was not really in the position to hire talent or to maintain the farm system and scouting crews necessary to ensure good new players. The factor that continued to hold the team in Cleveland was the money and determination of its newest owner, Francis O'Neill. A native-born Clevelander and avid sports fan, O'Neill was usually called Steve (after Steve O'Neill, catcher for the 1920s championship Indians and later the team's manager). When he bought the franchise in 1978, he vowed to make it solvent and, more important, to keep it in Cleveland. Keeping it in Cleveland turned out to be expensive, as O'Neill lost $10 to $12 million on the team. During this period he continually turned down lucrative offers that would have been to his advantage but would have resulted in the team's leaving the city. O'Neill's one-track civic vision was unusual in an era and a sports business not known for altruism. Only in the 1980s would O'Neill be partially recompensed for his troubles.

The problems of post-1960s Cleveland were also clearly reflected by the demise of professional hockey in the city. This sport, which had managed to struggle through the Depression, disappeared from Cleveland in 1978. During the 1950s the

Cleveland Browns Hall of Fame defensive end Len Ford during a November 1951 practice session. *Cleveland Press Collection, Cleveland State University.*

The CLEVELAND BARONS, formed in 1936 as charter members of the American Hockey League, played at the Cleveland Arena until leaving Cleveland in 1973. Initially owned by Al Sutphin, the Barons were perennial winners, capturing 9 regular-season titles and 8 Calder Cup playoff championships from 1940–51 to 1963–64, with the last championship team led by player/coach and Baron star Freddie Glover. From 1976 to 1978, a National Hockey League franchise christened the Barons played at the Richfield Coliseum, though the team finished last both years and merged with the NHL Minnesota North Stars.

Cleveland Barons had continued to play first-class minor-league hockey under the general management of Jackie Gordon. The sterling performance of player-coach Freddie Glover during this period was such that he was considered the team's greatest player. Under Glover's leadership, the team won the Calder Cup in 1963 and 1964. No matter how well the Barons played, however, they could not gain entry into the major National Hockey League. Attempts to do so in 1952 and 1968 were refused for reasons as varied as the relatively small seating capacity of the Arena and the poor attendance that had become typical at Cleveland hockey games by the 1960s. The league sensed that Cleveland was a minor- rather than a major-league hockey city.

In 1968, Nick Mileti purchased both the team and the Arena for $2 million. He

The Barons' 1962 front line (*left to right*) included Eldon Watson, Fred Hilts, player/coach Freddie Glover, Bill Masterson, and Pete Shearer. Glover led the team to its last Calder Cup in 1963–64. *Cleveland Press Collection, Cleveland State University.*

ARTHUR B. "ART" MODELL (23 June 1925–   ) bought the Cleveland Browns on 21 Mar. 1961 and began one of the National Football League's most successful continuous tenures of ownership. A competent administrator, Modell served as league president from 1967 to 1970. An early supporter of Monday night games, he volunteered the Browns to host the inaugural weeknight contest in 1970, and 85,703 packed Municipal Stadium to see the team defeat the New York Jets 31–21. In 1974, Modell signed a 25-year lease to maintain the Stadium, which in 1991 produced over $1 million in annual revenue for the city.

believed that he could make hockey work in Cleveland. Failing in his attempts to get the Barons into the major league, Mileti decided, in 1972, to purchase a franchise in the new World Hockey League. With the Cleveland Crusaders, the city at last had a major-league hockey team. But since it still had a minor-league team, the thin local hockey crowd was stretched even further. Attendance at Barons games plummeted to fewer than 1,000 fans per game. During its last game at the Arena, on January 8, 1973, the team drew only 412 people. Mileti then attempted to cut his losses and focus local attention on the Crusaders by moving the Barons to Jacksonville, Florida. The city was left with one team, the Crusaders, and, in 1974, with a new sports palace in which they could play. Built halfway between Cleveland and Akron in Richfield, Ohio, Nick Mileti's Coliseum was designed to draw crowds from both major cities. Its name was evocative of the sports empire Mileti was trying to build, as well as of the role that sports played in postwar America. It now seemed that with only one team to support and two cities to support it, hockey would survive in the Cleveland area. But attendance failed to increase sufficiently, and in 1976 Mileti moved the team to Hollywood, Florida.

There was to be one brief coda for professional hockey in Cleveland, however, when in 1976 Cleveland businessmen Mel Swig and George Gund III bought the failing San Francisco National Hockey League team, the Seals, and moved it to Cleveland, where it was rechristened the Barons. The city's only NHL team lasted two seasons before poor attendance forced its owners to merge it with the Minnesota North Stars.

The exact reason for the failure of hockey in Cleveland during the otherwise expansive American sports decade of the 1970s is difficult to ascertain. The most probable cause was the sport's relative unpopularity at that time, due in large part to the fact that it didn't "show" well on television. The fast-paced action left little time for commercials, and the small, hurtling puck was almost impossible to catch with the camera. At one point owners of the new World Hockey League franchises thought they could enhance the sport's TV image by using a colored puck. Cleveland, without a strong tradition of major-league hockey, did not have the critical mass of local support necessary to maintain a team through these difficult years. Other sports that televised well, particularly basketball, overshadowed hockey.

Basketball was one of the few success stories in Cleveland sports during the 1960–80 period. While Mileti may have failed to keep hockey in the city, he did succeed in creating the area's first long-lived professional basketball franchise.

Cleveland Browns majority owner Art Modell meets the press at the Browns training facility in Berea, Ohio, in 1989. *Courtesy of the* Plain Dealer.

JOHN B. McLENDON (5 Apr. 1915–   ) became the first black to coach professional basketball when the Cleveland Pipers joined the short-lived American Basketball League in 1961. McLendon joined the Pipers, an amateur team in the National Industrial Basketball League, in 1959 after coaching at North Carolina College and Tennessee A & I. George Steinbrenner acquired the Pipers in 1961 to be part of the new professional league. Even though the team did well, fan attendance was poor, and the coach left in mid-season. McLendon resumed his college coaching career, which included a brief stint at Cleveland State in the 1960s. He was voted into the National Association for Intercollegiate Athletics Hall of Fame and the Naismith Memorial Basketball Hall of Fame in 1978.

Mileti's Cleveland Cavaliers were admitted to the National Basketball Association during a league expansion in 1970. Staffed with college and expansion draftees, the team finished its first season with a dismal 15 and 67 record. In 1974, the team moved its games from the old Arena to the Coliseum. With constant improvement, occasioned largely by the talents of old pros such as Nate Thurmond, the Cavaliers proved to be a real national contender. In 1976 they won the Central Division championship of the NBA and went into the playoffs, where they eventually lost in

Cleveland Pipers coach John McLendon, the first black coach in professional basketball, discusses strategies with his players at a Pipers practice, 8 December 1959. *Cleveland Press Collection, Cleveland State University.*

HANK GREENBERG (1 Jan. 1911–2 Sept. 1986) served as the Cleveland Indians' general manager and managing partner (with Ellis Ryan) from 1950 to 1957. "High Henry" Greenberg was a Hall of Fame player (inducted in 1956) for the Detroit Tigers who appeared in 4 World Series (1934–35, 1940, 1945) and hit 331 home runs with a .313 career batting average. His greatest season as a player was in 1938, when he hit 58 home runs with 146 runs batted in. As an executive with the Indians, Greenberg helped to build the franchise during the 1950s; the 1954 team won 111 games, a league record.

the semifinals to the Boston Celtics. Mileti sold the team in 1980 and retired from local sports enterprises.

Moving the Cavaliers' home games to the Richfield Coliseum was part of what could be termed the suburbanization of sports. This followed the suburbanization of the population. Whereas in 1950 Cleveland's population constituted 66 percent of Cuyahoga County's, it fell to 38 percent of the county total in 1980. The largely white suburbs had one sports milieu, while the increasingly black and poor inner city had another. Indeed, it was charged that the Coliseum was created not only to

Indians General Manager Hank Greenberg "points out changes" in the ballclub to former owner Bill Veeck at the Indians' spring training in Tucson, Arizona, March 1954. *Cleveland Press Collection, Cleveland State University.*

draw crowds from both Cleveland and Akron but also to remove hockey and basketball from the Arena, which was situated on the largely black east side of Cleveland. After moving his teams from the Arena, Mileti tried to sell the structure. With no buyers, he had the building demolished in 1977.

The suburbanization of local sports was most apparent at the amateur level, both in recreational sports such as bowling, golf, and tennis, and in high-school sports. Golf and tennis, once the activities of the country club set, reached socioeconomically "downward" to attract an increasing number of players, while bowling, the workingman's pastime, moved upward in status.

The broad growth of interest and participation in golf began in the 1950s, spurred both by the additional time and money available to many Clevelanders and by the increasing recognition the sport began to gain through television broadcasts and the rise of several professional golf superstars. The era of public adulation for amateur golfers largely ended with Bobby Jones in the 1920s and 1930s. The careers of Walter Hagen during the 1920s and other professionals such as Ben Hogan and Sammy Snead in the following two decades heralded a new era in which professionals won all of the major open titles and recognition in the game. After 1933, for instance, no amateur golfer would again win the U.S. Open. One golfer in particular, with ties to Cleveland, would ensure the popularity of the game among a wide range of the population. Arnold Palmer, while stationed with the U.S. Coast Guard in Cleveland, won amateur recognition while playing at the local Pine Ridge Country Club. After turning professional in 1955, he went on to become one of the most successful and well-liked figures in sports. His success and popularity were, in large part, due to both his golfing ability and his amiable personality, which projected well during televised matches.

Cleveland Indians pitcher Bob Lemon delivers to the plate during the 1954 season. As a batter, the Hall of Fame pitcher hit 37 home runs in his career. *Cleveland Public Library.*

With time, money, and Palmer as an example, many Clevelanders began to take up the game. The number of local courses increased. In 1986 there were forty-four courses in metropolitan Cleveland and Cuyahoga County. Although a number remained as more or less exclusive private clubs, twenty-six were listed as open to the public. At the same time, various professional golf events were staged in the city. The Carling Open, held at Manakiki Country Club in 1953 and 1954, offered a mere $15,000 in combined prizes. By 1963, the Cleveland Open (which was discontinued in 1975) offered a purse of $100,000. Women's golf also prospered. Although gender-

biased clubs still denied voting privileges to women, the spouses of members played on many local private courses. Women's tournament golf grew under the guidance of the Ladies' Professional Golf Association. The first major tournament, the Babe Zaharias Invitational Classic, was played in Cleveland in 1976. Nationally, corporate sponsorships and increased prize monies pushed women's golf to higher levels of popularity, with players such as Nancy Lopez competing for $100,000+ prizes in tournaments such as the Dinah Shore Open.

Tennis was also affected by the suburbanization of local sports. Unlike golf, however, it did add a strong central city component by the 1970s. Like golf, tennis experienced a growth in popularity when the sport became increasingly professional and was televised. In the 1930s, players such as "Big Bill" Tilden had begun to turn professional. Tilden, however, could find little competition and earned little revenue from the matches he staged throughout the country. Even by the late 1940s, it was still difficult for players to find tournaments "open" to professionals as well as amateurs. By the 1950s matters began to change. Locally, John March, owner of the Shaker Racquet Club, began to stage tournaments for professionals. Nationally, the rise in the 1950s and 1960s of Australian pros such as Ken Rosewell and John Newcombe began to turn the game around. When Wimbledon became an open tournament in 1967, the major barrier had been breached. Television served as the prime catalyst in popularizing tennis. The amount of broadcast time devoted to the sport increased threefold during the period 1970–73 alone.

Inspired by both male and female (Virginia Wade and Chris Evert, for example) professional stars, Americans flocked to the tennis courts. In the early 1970s the number of tennis players in the United States quadrupled. In Cleveland and its suburbs, new courts were built at schools, and a large number of indoor "racquet" clubs were established in suburban areas as diverse as Valley View, Twinsburg, and Rocky River. With equipment costs less than those of golf, and with year-round indoor play available, the sport once fashionable on the lawns of Euclid Avenue mushroomed in popularity. In Cleveland, tennis had an important "inner-city" component. For many years the *Cleveland Press* and the *Plain Dealer* sponsored citywide junior tennis tournaments. Beginning in 1973, the National Junior Tennis League, formed by James and Sally Young, held summer training camps for inner-city youth at the Gordon and Rockefeller park courts. A decade later, the program was working with over 5,000 tennis players.

The city also developed a reputation as one of the most important international tennis centers during these two decades when many other local sports lost their luster. At the urging and under the leadership of Robert S. Malaga, Cleveland civic officials, and the Greater Cleveland Tennis Association, the Davis Cup matches came to the city in the 1960s and 1970s. In 1960, 1961, 1962, 1966, and 1979 the

This sequence details the grip and delivery used by Bob Feller when throwing a curve ball. Feller led the American League in strikeouts seven times and tossed three no-hitters. *Courtesy Del Bethel Collection.*

EARLY "GUS" WYNN, JR. (6 Jan 1920–   ) pitched for the Cleveland Indians from 1949 to 1957, and again in 1963. Beginning his career with the Washington Senators, Wynn came to the Indians in 1949, where he became part of the legendary pitching staff including Mike Garcia, Bob Feller, and Bob Lemon which would lead the Indians to a league record 111 victories in 1954. Wynn's 23 wins that season tied Lemon for the club lead. In his career, Wynn recorded 300 victories—164 for the Indians. He was elected to the Baseball Hall of Fame in 1971.

Indians pitcher Early "Gus" Wynn shakes hands with teammate Luke Easter after Wynn's complete-game victory, 6 August 1952. *Cleveland Press Collection, Cleveland State University.*

Mike Garcia of the Indians warms up prior to a game in 1950. *Cleveland Press Collection, Cleveland State University.*

EDWARD "MIKE" GARCIA (17 Nov. 1923–13 Jan. 1986) pitched for the Cleveland Indians from 1948 to 1956, averaging 20 victories a season from 1951 through 1954. He was a member of the Indians' "Big Four" starting pitchers, along with Bob Feller, Bob Lemon, and Early Wynn. In 14 seasons with the Indians, the Chicago White Sox, and the Washington Senators, Garcia had a won-loss record of 142–97.

LUSCIOUS "LUKE" EASTER (4 Aug. 1915–29 Mar. 1979) played first base for the Cleveland Indians from 1949 to 1954. Easter played in the Negro leagues with the Cincinnati Crescents in 1946 and the Homestead Grays in 1947–48 before Indians owner Bill Veeck signed him in 1949. Although he hit only 93 major-league home runs, Easter was notorious for tape-measure drives which radio announcer Jack Graney called "Bazooka Blasts." His 477-foot home run on 23 June 1950 landed in the upper deck, the longest ever hit at Municipal Stadium. Easter, murdered in 1979, served as director of the Cleveland Baseball Federation and is memorialized by a scholarship at Cleveland State University.

American zone finals were played in the city. The world finals came to Cleveland in 1964, 1969 and 1970, and 1973, and interzone matches were held locally in 1968. The same civic activism on the part of Malaga and civic leaders brought the Wightman Cup matches between United States and British women to Cleveland in 1963, 1965, 1967, 1969, 1971, and 1975. In addition, Cleveland hosted women's matches between Australia and the United States in 1972 and 1974, as well as the Western Open.

By the mid-1970s, tennis had become such a major draw that promoters decided

Indians first baseman Luscious "Luke" Easter watches one fly for a long out, 20 April 1950. *Cleveland Press Collection, Cleveland State University.*

ROCCO DOMENICO "ROCKY" COLAVITO (10 Aug. 1933–) was an outfielder with the Cleveland Indians from 1955 to 1959 and from 1965 to 1967. He led the American League with 42 home runs in 1959 but was traded to Detroit the next year. After 4 years with the Tigers and a year with Kansas City, he returned to the Indians in 1965 and led the league in RBIs with 108. He played briefly with the Chicago and New York clubs in the American League and Los Angeles in the National League. In his 14-year major-league career, Colavito hit 374 home runs.

it too should become a team sport. Established by noted female tennis star Billie Jean King, her husband Larry, and sports entrepreneur Dennis Murphy, the World Team Tennis League came into existence in 1973. Local promoter Joe Zingale thought that team tennis would prosper in Cleveland, and in 1974 he bought a franchise which he named the Cleveland Nets. During their four-year tenure in the city, the Nets featured a wealth of talent, including the city's most famous tennis player, Clark Graebner (who served as player-coach), Marty Riessen, Martina Navratilova, and a young Bjorn Borg. The franchise never had a winning season (which consisted of forty-four matches), but it did manage to make the playoffs twice. Initially playing at Public Hall, the Nets moved to the Coliseum in 1975. This improved their attendance, which had hovered around 50,000 per season, but making a profit still proved difficult. In an attempt to boost attendance, Zingale began to search for star attractions. In 1977 he signed both Bjorg and noted transsexual player Renee Richards. He also scheduled some of the team's home games in other cities, including Pittsburgh, St. Louis, Miami, and New Orleans. Neither the home game moves nor the signing of Richards could keep the Nets in the city. During this last "home" season, with all of its money-making ploys, the team managed only a $165,000 profit, of which $125,000 was due to a trade. Zingale moved the team to New Orleans in 1978, the year in which the league collapsed. Obituaries for team

(LEFT) **Rocky Colavito resigns with the Indians after a five-year absence on 10 February 1965.** *Cleveland Public Library.*

(RIGHT) **Indians outfielder Rocky Colavito robs the Washington Senators' Paul Casanova of a home run, 27 May 1967.** *Cleveland Public Library.*

FRANK LANE (1 Feb. 1896–20 Mar. 1981) served as general manager and executive vice-president of the Cleveland Indians from 1958 to 1960. Known in Cleveland as "Trader" Lane because of his penchant for swapping players, he was the object of city ridicule after the trades of first baseman Norm Cash and outfielder Rocky Colavito to the Detroit Tigers in April 1960. Lane once estimated that he worked over 300 deals involving 700 players during his career, which saw him employed by 8 major-league teams from 1933 until the early 1970s.

tennis remarked on the fact that despite the broadening appeal of the game, the partisan crowd atmosphere cut against the grain of the sport.

While tennis and golf filtered downward through the community, bowling acquired more status. The sport had seen tremendous growth during the 1940s, when bowling alleys near defense plants catered to huge numbers of workers. Industries were encouraged to sponsor industrial league teams to boost worker morale. The sport grew spectacularly as the number of bowling centers in Cleveland rose from 59 in 1939 to 106 in 1945. Youngsters were encouraged to bowl, and during the war a Cleveland interscholastic bowling league was formed. Black participation in the sport also increased, but in bowling as elsewhere, discrimination was the rule; African-Americans were barred from membership in the American Bowling Congress and the Women's International Bowling Congress. To counter this,

Indians fans scream for Frank Lane's "removal" at the Stadium after the announcement of the trade of popular Indians player Rocky Colavito on 19 April 1960. *Cleveland Press Collection, Cleveland State University.*

Indians fans line up for their cheap drafts on Beer Night at Municipal Stadium in 1971. *Cleveland Press Collection, Cleveland State University.*

An injured fan is escorted away by an umpire during Dime Beer Night at the Stadium, 6 June 1974. The raucous crowd forced an Indians forfeit. *Cleveland Press Collection, Cleveland State University.*

Clevelander J. Elmer Reed helped establish the National Negro Bowling Association and, locally, the Cleveland Bowling Senate. In 1950, following a lawsuit, the ABC and the WBC opened membership to blacks.

The invention of the automatic pinsetter in 1946 by American Machine and Foundry (AMF) changed the game forever by speeding up pinsets, making them more accurate, and cutting the labor costs associated with pinboys. Sensing an increasing market, bowling proprietors began to build new alleys. Many were in suburban areas. The new alleys had none of the barroom atmosphere of the alleys of old. Complete with pro shops, cocktail lounges, soda fountains, and, in some cases, babysitters, they catered to a more affluent suburban clientele. Even at a construction cost of $50,000 per lane, many of the new "bowling centers" (the use of the term *alley*, with its negative connotations, was being discouraged by this time) turned a profit. By the mid-1970s over 100,000 Cleveland-area residents bowled in sanctioned leagues sponsored by businesses, labor unions, industries, clubs, and other organizations. An additional 200,000 recreational and nonsanctioned league bowlers also used the facilities. Much of the increased participation came from women, whose numbers in the sport had doubled since the early 1950s, as well as from businessmen. Bowling was no longer a predominantly male, blue-collar activity.

As with other sports, television served to popularize the game. Its professional component grew rapidly as Clevelanders watched matches televised on Sunday afternoons. The Professional Bowlers Association, established in 1958, sponsored a national tour. Cleveland became a regular stop on the tour in 1974. Bowling certainly had not risen to the level of an elite sport, but it was attracting a large clientele from what had become a leisure-rich local population.

There were few really elite sports left in Cleveland by the 1960s and 1970s. The value of golf and tennis as status symbols was somewhat lessened by the movement of the middle class into these games. Private country clubs could, of course, keep their courses exclusive. And the tennis courts at sites such as the Country Club and the Kirtland Club could maintain a certain tone, one that certainly differed from that at the public courts found in locations such as the Flats near Jennings Road, or

FREDDIE GLOVER (5 Jan. 1928–   ) played hockey for the Cleveland Barons for 15 seasons and in 1958 was appointed player/coach by owner Paul Bright. He led the Barons to one last Calder Cup championship in 1963–64. Glover set American Hockey League all-time records in goals (scoring 520 goals in his career), assists, points, and penalty minutes. Playing in the National Hockey League for two years with Detroit and Chicago early in his career, Glover coached the California Golden Seals from 1968 to 1971 and the Los Angeles Kings for the 1971–72 season.

on the lakefront, cheek-by-jowl with the Shoreway and the Division Avenue Filtration Plant. There were upscale alternatives to tennis, however, for by the 1970s new vogues including squash and platform tennis became fashionable among the city's higher-income citizens. Even horseracing lost its remaining exclusivity in the 1950s. The crowds that went to the Randall and Thistledown tracks represented all elements of society. The horsemen of the city no longer congregated at the Roadside Club, but at the Theatrical, the Grogshop, Kornman's Restaurant, and other bars and restaurants on Cleveland's notorious and colorful Short Vincent Street. The congregants at the Short Vincent watering holes, who during the 1940s and 1950s included Bill Veeck and other sports figures, and were styled as the "Jolly Set," were

Freddie Glover of the Cleveland Barons (#9) gets off a shot against Providence while falling to the ice in November 1964 American Hockey League action. *Cleveland Press Collection, Cleveland State University.*

NICK MILETI (22 Apr. 1931–   ), a native Clevelander, organized a group of investors and sought to build a sports empire in Cleveland from 1968 to 1980. They purchased the Cleveland Barons and the Cleveland Arena in 1968 and the Cleveland Indians in 1972. The holdings were expanded when Mileti organized the Cleveland Cavaliers and the short-lived Cleveland Crusaders hockey team, and he built the Richfield Coliseum, where the teams played. Radio station WWWE was acquired to broadcast the clubs' baseball, basketball, and hockey games. Mileti left Cleveland for California in 1980. Although none of his teams achieved the success he hoped for, the Coliseum and the Cavaliers remain as his legacy.

willing to give odds on almost any sport, but particularly on horses. Those odds spanned races across the country as well as the day's races at Thistledown and North Randall.

Ironically, while the denizens of Short Vincent were betting on the thorough-

Nick Mileti and his first big investment in the Cleveland sports scene: the Cleveland Arena, ca. 1969. *Cleveland Press Collection, Cleveland State University.*

The RICHFIELD COLISEUM, in Summit County, was built in 1973 by Cleveland entrepreneur Nick Mileti at a cost of $32 million. Home of the National Basketball Association Cleveland Cavaliers and the Major Soccer League Cleveland Crunch, as well as the 1976–78 National Hockey League Cleveland Barons, the Coliseum also hosts other sporting events—professional wrestling, Olympic tours, and truck pulls. The dimensions of the Coliseum (12 stories high, 475 feet by 350 feet), plus a seating capacity of 20,000, allow the complex to host major concerts, trade shows, and exhibitions.

breds at Thistledown, harness racing returned to the area when Northfield Track opened in 1957. Northfield, however, was not the Glenville track, and the patrons and owners did not include the descendants of Millionaires' Row. Instead, the track tried to capitalize on a new interest in harness racing. As was the case with trotting tracks across the country, Northfield's owner, Walter J. Michael, and after 1972 owners Carl Milstein, Robert Stakich, and George Steinbrenner, tried to do away with the "old fogey" image of trotting. Drivers began to wear helmets and tight-fitting uniforms to impart a sense of speed and daring to the sport, and betting was encouraged in order to increase excitement. Despite a growth in attendance, how-

Sports entrepreneur Nick Mileti stands outside the Richfield Coliseum during construction in January 1974. *Cleveland Public Library.*

Arnold Palmer and the gallery react as Palmer misses a close putt at the 1964 Cleveland Open. *Cleveland Press Collection, Cleveland State University.*

ever, the trotters at Northfield lost money during the 1970s and into the 1980s. Only a state tax break for the racing industry in 1984 kept the track in business.

Polo remained perhaps the only elite sport in Cleveland during the postwar period, although by this time the teams were not necessarily composed of the scions of wealthy families but of excellent amateur players from a variety of backgrounds. It was the tone of the crowd that now gave status to the game. Following a wartime hiatus, William Herbert Greene organized a new local team in 1950. In 1953 he went on to establish the Cleveland Polo Association. The 200 members of the group helped support the team. By 1960, however, the members of the association appeared to be the only spectators for polo, with game attendance averaging about 200. By 1964 there were two four-man teams playing in the area, and attendance at matches at the Metroparks Polo Field had risen to about 3,000. Eventually, by the early 1980s, the area would have only one team, the Shamrocks, who in that year

Rumanian tennis stars Ilie Nastase and Ion Kiriac (future coach of German superstar Boris Becker) are seen here in action from 1969 Davis Cup competition in Cleveland, 19 September 1969. *Cleveland Press Collection, Cleveland State University.*

The CLEVELAND NETS (1974–1977) were the local franchise of the short-lived World Team Tennis league. Clevelander Joe Zingale bought the franchise for $50,000 and set about signing players to exclusive contracts, including Mary Riessen (player/coach 1975–77 and 1975 Rookie of the Year), Martina Navratilova (1976), and Bjorn Borg (1977). The Nets played their first season at Public Hall, then moved to the Richfield Coliseum in 1975. However, their inability to finish over .500 and poor attendance prompted Zingale to move the team to New Orleans in Feb. 1978.

Cleveland Nets players Marty Riessen and Haroon Rahim (*behind net*) confront Vitas Gerulaitus and Mark Cox over a controversial call in their July 1976 World Team Tennis match. *Cleveland Press Collection, Cleveland State University.*

An instructor demonstrates the proper follow-through to his attentive students at the "Bowling Institute," held at Benedictine High School in the late 1940s. *Cleveland Press Collection, Cleveland State University.*

won the Mid-State Championship, the first polo title for a local team in twenty years.

Although the general spread of once-exclusive sports through broad segments of the population could be taken as a sign of wealth and civic well-being, not all was well in the city or in its sports community during the 1960s and 1970s. Rather, there was increasing impoverishment in the inner city and growing racial confrontation in the community. These problems were echoed to an extent in local sports. While

Northfield Lanes, shown here in 1961, was one of many "Bowling Centers" around metropolitan Cleveland to emerge after the 1940s as the sport's popularity gained a suburban foothold. *Cleveland Press Collection, Cleveland State University.*

Trotters round the first turn at Northfield Park, where year-round harness racing makes its home in northeast Ohio, ca. 1990. *Northfield Park.*

the declining fortunes of major teams such as the Indians, the demise of hockey, and the shift of arena sports to the suburban Coliseum mirrored the economic situation of the city, the state of municipal and high-school athletics most graphically illustrated the divisions and poverty within Cleveland.

The demise of the annual charity football game was a case in point. At one time the contest was almost certain to draw more than 19,000 spectators annually to the Municipal Stadium. In 1946, a crowd of 70,955 viewed a charity game between Holy Name and Cathedral Latin. By the 1960s, however, attendance began to dwindle, and the behavior of those who did come created problems. Postgame assaults, vandalism in the downtown area, and what the *Cleveland Press* called "hoodlumism in broad daylight" became common. After some members of the 1969 crowd broke windows at downtown stores, the councilman for that area, Gerald McFaul, called for cancellation of the game. The 1970 game was canceled, not only because of the violence but because the gate receipts now barely paid for rental of the stadium.

During the late 1960s, the major parochial high schools in Cleveland began to withdraw their teams from the Athletic Senate. Citing financial losses because of poor attendance during league play, schools such as Cathedral Latin left the senate

NORTHFIELD PARK, located on Rt. 8, was opened in 1957 to capitalize on the renewed interest in harness racing. The track was constructed by Walter J. Michael of Bucyrus, head of the U.S. Trotting Association. The half-mile track begins in Summit County, turns into Cuyahoga County, and ends again in Summit. By the 1990s the facility was open year-round, with 213 racing dates, of which 35 were daytime events. The glass-enclosed clubhouse and grandstand allowed for winter viewing, and the average attendance for the 1989–90 season was 3,474.

JOHN S. NAGY (1913–27 July 1983) served four decades as commissioner of recreation in Cleveland (1943–1983). Nagy had a distinguished sports career at Ohio State University, which included boxing, football, and baseball. He became assistant commissioner of recreation for Cleveland in 1939, and in 1943 assumed the commissioner's post. His office administered swimming pools, baseball diamonds, golf courses, and skating rinks and augmented recreational activities for youth, with summer employment opportunities at these facilities. Nagy also served as president of the Lake Erie AAU, host of the local Golden Gloves boxing tournament. He retired in 1983.

as early as 1968. Benedictine, Holy Name, and St. Ignatius followed suit, withdrawing, respectively, in 1972, 1975, and 1979. After the public schools were ordered to desegregate in 1976, additional pressure was placed on high-school teams. Busing students to achieve racial balance had enormous effects on traditional rivalries as, for better or for worse, student bodies no longer represented neighborhoods but academic institutions. The vigor and the venom that had been part of regional rivalries were lost. In 1979, the senate was reorganized into north and south divisions, as the former east and west division was too suggestive of the racial alignment of the city, with a large black east side population and a predominantly white west side population. Creating still more difficulty for public high-school athletics was the declining student population. The drop in the number of students followed the city's own loss of population, of course, but it also came from a huge high-school dropout rate—approaching 50 percent of total enrollment by the 1980s. Cleveland public school athletic coaches no longer had access to the large pool of talent that had once made possible great teams such as those fielded by John Marshall in football or East Tech in basketball.

The municipal recreation program, administered with devotion and care by John Nagy, the city's recreation commissioner from 1943 to 1983, also suffered as the city lost population, industry, and the resultant tax revenues necessary to maintain parks and playgrounds. While hockey, basketball, Golden Gloves boxing, and indoor sports continued at local recreation centers, the city's once-vaunted sandlot fields at Edgewater, Gordon, and Garfield parks fell into disrepair. Eventually, in 1978, a lease agreement between the city and the state transferred control of Gordon and Edgewater parks to the state, which had sufficient funds to improve and maintain the facilities. Garfield Park, which suffered even greater damage from neglect and vandalism, would not be rescued until 1986, when it was acquired by the Cleveland Metroparks System.

Perhaps worst among the city's misfortunes of the 1960s and 1970s was its seeming inability to heal its racial divisions. Despite the promising beginnings in the immediate postwar period, the city continued to be divided along black and white lines into the 1960s. Housing shortages, unemployment, and educational overcrowding led to a series of local civil rights protests in 1963. Eventually the Hough riots and the Glenville shootout would add Cleveland's name to the list of American cities that had suffered urban rioting. At this same time, American sports con-

Cleveland Commissioner of Recreation John S. Nagy (*right*) purchases a Municipal Hockey Night ticket from a young participant, ca. 1950. *Cleveland Public Library.*

Promoter Don King and heavyweight champion Mike Tyson (*in hat*) share a laugh at a Cleveland press conference in 1989. *The* Plain Dealer.

tinued to confront the issue of racism. Although black athletes had been participating in all major sports for over a decade, there was still discrimination, both subtle and overt, practiced at some major colleges (particularly in the South), as well as within the clubhouse. As some African-Americans achieved notice and prominence within the sporting community, they used that forum to protest the general conditions of their race throughout the nation. Boxing heavyweight champion Muhammad Ali was perhaps the most visible symbol of black pride and protest during the era. The most dramatic event during this time was the protest staged by runners Tommy Smith and John Carlos on the victory platform at the 1968 Mexico City Olympics, when they raised their fists in a "black power" salute during the playing of the American national anthem.

Locally, nothing as dramatic occurred, despite the fact that there were racial overtones to some sports-related activities. Many Cleveland blacks felt that the construction of the Coliseum in Richfield was an affront, an attempt both to remove them as spectators from the Arena and to move the facility away from the "undesirable" inner city. Fault was also found with the placement and maintenance of pools and sporting facilities in the city's black neighborhoods. Nevertheless, Cleveland's professional sports teams attempted to continue away from bias, a move that had begun with the signing of players such as Motley, Doby, and Willis. The Cleveland Pipers' hiring of John McLendon as the nation's first black professional basketball coach, and the Cleveland Indians' signing of Frank Robinson in 1974 as the first black major-league baseball coach were certainly steps that continued in the right direction. In boxing, local fight promoter Don King moved the African-American presence beyond the ring itself as he successfully promoted several major fights locally, including the Muhammad Ali–Chuck Wepner title bout of 1975, and then went on to become one of the nation's major fight promoters. In the 1980s, King would try to convince one of his champions, Mike Tyson, to take up residence in Cleveland. However, the one local black athletic figure who towered above all others as both symbol and spokesman during the post-1960 period was Jim Brown, fullback for what was the most admired sports team in the city during that period. Brown was a spokesman for civil rights and a symbol of black pride, as well as a consummate athlete.

FRANK D. ROBINSON (31 Aug. 1935–   ) was the player-manager of the Cleveland Indians from 1975 to 1977, the first black ever to serve as manager in the major leagues. Robinson was National League Rookie of the Year in 1956 with the Cincinnati Reds and NL Most Valuable Player in 1962. He won the Triple Crown with the Baltimore Orioles in 1965, batting .316 with 49 home runs and 122 runs batted in—for which he was named the American League MVP, the only player so honored in both leagues. Named to the Hall of Fame in 1982, Robinson has also served as manager for the San Francisco Giants and the Baltimore Orioles.

While the Indians and other local teams faltered, the Browns' popularity continued to grow, with the team frequently filling the 80,000-seat stadium for its home games. Despite Art Modell's controversial firing of head coach Paul Brown in 1963, the team managed to continue its winning ways. The extraordinary talent of Jim Brown contributed much to this success. During his nine years with the Browns, he won the NFL rushing title seven times and set a lifetime rushing record that would not be eclipsed until 1984. Under new coach Blanton Collier, the team won the NFL championship in 1964 and managed to gain its divisional title during each of the next four seasons. When the National Football League merged with the American Football League in 1970, the Browns became a member of the new Central Division, as did arch-rival Pittsburgh. The team gained playoff status under new (1971) coach Nick Skorich in 1971 and 1972. The reign of Forrest Gregg as head coach from 1975 to 1977 produced no playoff berths, but the next coach, Sam Rutigliano, managed to get the team to a division title during his first year, 1978, and into the playoffs in 1981. Certainly the Browns did not have the consistent winning record they had enjoyed during the late 1940s and early 1950s, but they played head-and-shoulders above the other local teams. Only they seemed to keep the city's spirits high during the dismal decades of the 1960s and 1970s.

City and Sports Renaissance? The 1980s

Entrepreneurs such as Nick Mileti who wheeled and dealed in local sports in the 1970s were riding the crest of a new economic wave. Mileti, George and Gordon Gund, and later Richard and David Jacobs realized that sports were no longer a pastime, or even a good side investment, but an integral part of the evolving service economy in America. Nationally, the growth of leisure time and, particularly, television had much to do with this trend. American's hunger for sports was reflected in their television viewing habits. By the 1960s, what had been single broadcasts of events such as baseball games, the Friday night fights, and football games were supplemented by sports programming such as the "Wide World of Sports" and, a decade later, "Monday Night Football." If a sport couldn't be televised, it stood to fail; such was the case of the World Football League, which collapsed after two years because of a lack of television coverage and revenues. As television contracts filled

Cleveland Indian Player-Manager Frank Robinson, the first black manager in baseball history, leads the ballclub from the dugout in 1975. *Cleveland Indians Baseball Club; Photo by Paul Tepley.*

the coffers of the owners, players began to demand and get more of the proceeds. By 1981, the average salary in the National Basketball Association had reached $200,000, largely because of a bidding war with the new rival American Basketball Association. When, after nearly 100 years, baseball's reserve clause was invalidated in 1975, and the players could become free agents, salaries rose from an average $44,000 to $110,000 in only four years. To the youngster watching the professional games, athletes now more than ever signified wealth and status in addition to skill. To entrepreneurs looking at a growing television audience, including those viewing on the all-sports cable network ESPN (introduced in 1979), sports, despite the high salaries, still meant substantial profits.

JIM BROWN (17 Feb. 1936–   ) played running back for the Cleveland Browns from 1957 to 1965. Considered by many to be the greatest National Football League running back ever, the overpowering Brown collected 8 NFL rushing titles in his 9-year career and set records in yards gained in a season (1,883), career rushing yards (12,312), combined yardage in rushing and receiving (15,459), rushing attempts (2,359), yards per carry (5.2), and touchdowns scored (126). A 3-time NFL MVP, in 1964 Brown led the Browns to their only NFL title. He was inducted into the Hall of Fame in 1971.

Cleveland entered the 1980s having just come out of fiscal default (in 1978 it was the first major American city to default on its fiscal obligations since the Depression) with the realization that its old industrial economy was no longer viable. Service industries such as banks, hospitals, restaurants, entertainment, and hotels would now be the core of the economy. Sports would be a critical ingredient in two ways: Winning teams would not only boost the city's image through their national exposure, but also bring needed revenues to the community. The place of sports in civic life had come 180 degrees from its origins. Play was now work, and sporting pastimes were economic products of equal or greater value than previous products such as agricultural crops, or the iron and steel produced by Cleveland's once vast mills. By the end of the decade, many believed the city had achieved a renaissance as it escaped default. New construction projects filled the downtown area, and Cleveland earned national recognition as an "All American City."

As was the case in the late 1940s, success on the part of the city's professional

(LEFT) **Legendary Browns running back Jim Brown eludes a Philadelphia Eagles defender during a December 1958 game.** *Cleveland Press Collection, Cleveland State University.*

(RIGHT) **Browns Hall of Fame wide receiver Paul Warfield gathers in a pass in December 1968. The Warren, Ohio, native had a career 20.1-yard-per-catch average, highest in NFL history.** *Cleveland Press Collection, Cleveland State University.*

teams seemed to echo this rebirth; however, none went so far as to win a national title. This alone might have called into question the solidity of the "urban renaissance."

Nationally, baseball seemed to regain much of its lost luster in the 1980s; it was once again hailed as the national pastime during an era when the presidency of Ronald Reagan prompted Americans to look back to the days of traditional national values. Movies such as *The Natural* and *Field of Dreams* added to the renewed infatuation with the game. During the first half of the decade, it appeared that the Indians would let down the city and those who again looked to baseball as an exciting, rewarding pastime. By 1985 there was new talk of moving the team out of town when it slid to last place with an appalling 60 and 102 record, the worst in modern baseball. It was, at that time, $11 million in debt. However, the O'Neill family, which had maintained ownership after Steve's death in 1983, refused to move the Indians. In 1986 the team rebounded with an exciting season and a finish above .500. Attendance climbed to 1.5 million that year, and the city had seemingly once again caught "Indians Fever." Later that year the O'Neill heirs agreed to sell the club to Richard E. and David H. Jacobs for more than $30 million, after being convinced of the Jacobses' intention to keep the Indians in Cleveland. During the remainder of the decade the Indians would ride a roller coaster of good starts and bad finishes, but the renewed interest in the sport served to keep crowd figures relatively high.

Like the Indians, the Cleveland Cavaliers began the 1980s in poor form. Under the ownership of local sports promoter Ted Stepian from 1980 to 1983, the club faltered as a result of poor trades and less-than-inspired play. It finished the 1981–82 season with a disastrous 15 and 67 record. By the end of his tenure, Stepian found himself selling players to keep the franchise solvent. Altogether, his ill-fated ownership of the team cost him $15 million over three years. His sale of the Cavaliers to George and Gordon Gund, sons of George Gund, prominent banker, businessman, and brewer's son, led to a new era that remarkably paralleled changes taking place in the city. The Gunds installed new management and in 1986 turned over the general management and coaching of the team to two African-Americans, Wayne

Cleveland real estate developers David (*left*) and Richard Jacobs purchased the Indians in 1986 with the intention of keeping the team in Cleveland, relieving anxious Tribe fans around the city. *The* Plain Dealer.

Embry and Lenny Wilkens. Embry and Wilkens belonged to and symbolized the evolving black upper-middle class in Greater Cleveland, and their efforts were instrumental in making the team one of the most successful local professional franchises.

One of the unexpected professional sports successes in the city during 1980s was indoor soccer. A fast-paced game more suited to American tastes than traditional European football, the indoor version attracted a suburban, upper-middle-class crowd. The Cleveland Force debuted in 1978 under the ownership of Eric Henderson. A shaky first season resulted in a 5 and 19 record, and Henderson had to sell the team. The new owners, Bart Wolstein and his son Scott, saw the club become a contender in the Major Indoor Soccer League and begin to produce profits. After 1982 the Wolsteins set about acquiring the best players available. The results were impressive. The Force reached the league playoffs in 1982, 1983, 1985, and 1986, although they never won the championship. The excitement generated by the team drew nearly 400,000 people to its games at the Richfield Coliseum in the mid-1980s. By 1988, the Force was disbanded as the Major Indoor Soccer League succumbed to fiscal problems. Local interest remained strong, however, and in 1989 George Hoffmann and Stuart Lichter created a new team, the Cleveland Crunch, to play in the new Major Soccer League.

Football remained the most highly patronized and successful local sport during the city's renaissance. The early 1980s were less than memorable for the Browns. A poor beginning to the 1984 season led Art Modell to fire the coach, Sam Rutigliano. Under new coach Marty Schottenheimer, the team improved, winning the Central Division title in 1986. Advancing into the playoffs that year and each succeeding year through 1989, the Browns created an aura of excitement during the fall and winter months. Quarterback Bernie Kosar, a product of nearby Poland, Ohio, was the object of adulation on and off the field. Staid citizens barked like dogs to celebrate the team's "Dawg [dogged] Defense." Despite reaching the playoffs, the last-minute victories, and the huge outpouring of support, the Browns always failed at their ultimate goal, a place in football's Super Bowl championship game. Having led

Cavaliers center Larry Nance blocks Michael Jordon's lay-up attempt as the Cavs wrangled with the Chicago Bulls in a 1989 game. *The* Plain Dealer.

the team far, but not far enough, Coach Schottenheimer was fired at the end of the 1989 season.

The city's avidity for professional sports was duplicated in its citizens' pursuit of amateur sport in the 1980s. Golf and tennis continued to be popular, as did bowling, but new activities came to the forefront. Softball, in particular, expanded greatly in this decade.

Softball had been played in the city since the 1920s. In the 1930s, I. S. "Nig" Rose of the Cleveland Baseball Federation reformed the game, giving it baseball rules and creating the Cleveland Municipal Softball Association to oversee the leagues that formed. Both slow-pitch and fast-pitch softball could, like hardball, be played with skill, fervor, and energy, but they could also be more casual sports suited to the weekend athlete. By the 1950s, the game was spreading rapidly throughout Cleveland, as factories, unions, and businesses formed teams. Teams such as the one sponsored by the Pyramid Cafe came to dominate the local sport, and by the 1960s and 1970s, local diamonds, once the site of fast-pitch sandlot ball, were hosting softball games. Morgana Park on the city's southeast side was perhaps the principal venue for industrial softball games in Cleveland. The sport also grew rapidly in the suburbs, with many teams being sponsored by local taverns. The possibilities for entrepreneurship in the game were not lost as businesses eagerly sponsored teams for name exposure. Promoter Ted Stepian capitalized on this growing popularity by opening a set of fields for hire under the name "Softball World" in suburban Brook Park. The fields' location, hard by local Chevrolet and Ford plants, said much about who had the major interest in the sport.

Perhaps the preeminent amateur sport in Cleveland during the 1970s and 1980s was running. Jogging and marathon running, spurred in part by a growing societal interest in a healthful lifestyle, could involve both sexes and nearly all ages. Locally, the Revco Marathon, which drew 250 runners to its first race in 1976, grew into an event with international representation and 13,000 runners only ten years later. The Bonne Bell Run, sponsored by a local cosmetics manufacturer, was only a 10-kilo-

Cavaliers general manager Wayne Embry presents Cavs coach Lenny Wilkins with a cup commemorating Wilkins's 600th victory as an NBA coach, on 12 January 1988. *Courtesy Cleveland Cavaliers.*

The CLEVELAND FORCE pro indoor soccer team was one of Cleveland's most successful modern sports franchises. The Force debuted in 1978 with the Major Indoor Soccer League. After an inaugural season record of 5–19, the franchise was bought out by Bart and Scott Wolstein. By 1983, the team had acquired such top players as Kai Haaskivi. Although the Force was an annual play-off participant, with Coliseum crowds averaging 12,000, money losses and league contract squabbles compelled Bart Wolstein to fold the team after the 1987–88 season.

meter race, rather than a marathon, but it too grew with the increasing interest in running. Running was so popular in some city suburbs that joggers began vying with automobiles for road space. The city of Shaker Heights became sufficiently concerned about potential accidents to post pictographs of joggers along the popular Shaker Lakes jogging routes. Bicycling also benefited from the national interest in a healthful, active lifestyle in the 1970s, ending a hiatus begun in the 1920s when Americans gave up their two-wheelers for cars. It seemed that between the 1920s and 1970s, the only people in Cleveland with bicycles were those too young to drive.

Ian Anderson of the Cleveland Force sits on the floor after scoring as teammate Ruben Astigarraga (#23) rushes to congratulate him, 25 February 1981. *Cleveland Press Collection, Cleveland State University.*

KAI HAASKIVI (28 Dec. 1955–   ), professional indoor soccer star and Lahti, Finland, native, was a member of the defunct Cleveland Force and in 1991 played for the Cleveland Major Soccer League franchise, the Crunch. Haaskivi, a four-time Major Indoor Soccer League first-team selection, was recognized as a member of the MISL 1980's All-Decade Team. After six seasons with the Force, Haaskivi returned to Cleveland in 1989 to serve as Crunch player/coach. Haaskivi is the career leader in nearly all Force/Crunch offensive categories, and is the only Cleveland player with a retired number (12).

Running and cycling were two of the major athletic events in which women could compete. Although Title IX of the Educational Amendment Act of 1972 provided a tremendous boost to women's scholastic athletic programs by prohibiting gender discrimination within federally funded institutions, the presence of women on the overall sports scene remained secondary. Popular, lucrative professional sports careers for women remained confined largely to the tennis courts and golf courses. An attempt to establish a national Women's Basketball League in 1978 failed when the league collapsed three years later. Local women's physical education teachers had long tried to increase recognition of women's athletics. In 1943 they founded the Cleveland Women's Physical Education and Recreation Association, which evolved into an organization dedicated to providing a lobbying group and forum for women interested in physical education, recreation, and related fields. Title IX did fulfill some of their hopes as it led to a rapid evolution of women's basketball on both the high-school and the college level in Cleveland, and increased opportunity for females in track and field, much to the delight of female coaches

(LEFT) **Cleveland Crunch star Kai Haaskivi (***left***) and a Crunch teammate race after a loose ball in a 1990 exhibition match.** *Photo by Ken Sarnecki, courtesy of the Cleveland Crunch.*

(RIGHT) **Midfielder David Hoggin of the Crunch clears the ball in a 1990 game against the St. Louis Storm.** *Photo by Ken Sarnecki, courtesy of the Cleveland Crunch.*

The CLEVELAND CRUNCH of the renamed Major Soccer League filled the void created by the demise of the Major Indoor Soccer League Cleveland Force. Granted an expansion franchise in February 1989 by the renamed Major Soccer League, owners George Hoffman and Stuart Lichter created a high-caliber team led by player/coach Kai Haaskivi, the former Force standout. Following an inaugural season record of 20–32 at the Richfield Coliseum in 1989–90, the 1990–91 Crunch captured the MSL Eastern Division title with a record of 29–23.

and former track stars such as Frances Kaszubski and Maralyn West, who had labored for nearly thirty years in an attempt to get more attention for women's track and field.

Kaszubski, who had participated in basketball and track and field (where the discus was her favorite event) and worked in the city's recreation department, waged a long and effective campaign to earn national and international recognition for women's track and field. Her management of the 1960 American women's Olympic track-and-field team led not only to a successful Olympics for the team, but also to an increased interest in women's track.

Although women's athletics were, by virtue of Title IX, a large part of the local high-school sports programs in the 1980s, here, too, women's basketball, baseball, and other activities were still overshadowed by men's varsity sports. Whereas in the 1940s and 1950s the great contests and rivalries involved teams from city schools, both public and parochial, in the 1980s much of the attention paid to high-school sports was focused on suburban schools. Several city parochial schools, including St. Ignatius and Benedictine, continued to field extraordinary teams in basketball and football. Coach Augie Bossu's nearly forty-year tenure at Benedictine, where he used football to turn out "good Christian men" and in the process turned out winning football teams, continued through the 1980s. Benedictine captured the state championships in 1973 and 1980. Across town, St. Ignatius won the title in 1988 and 1989. Wrestling, reduced professionally to staged theatrics, had its only true venues in the scholastic arena. Wrestling had been established in the high schools in the 1920s, and a statewide wrestling tournament had evolved by 1939. Locally, the sport grew tremendously after World War II. By the 1970s and 1980s, it too was dominated by the suburban high schools, most notably by the St. Edwards of Lakewood teams, coached by Howard Ferguson, and those of Maple Heights, coached by Mike Milkovich.

With scholastic athletics seen increasingly by many as a step to lucrative professional careers, and as juvenile versions of the big leagues, the competition between schools was carefully regulated to provide for equality of play. By 1990 a series of divisions had been created throughout the state, which matched schools with similar enrollment levels against each other. Five divisions demarcated local football competition, basketball was organized into four divisions, and wrestling and baseball into three. Cutting across division lines were a series of leagues set up to allow for easy travel within the various suburban areas of Cleveland. Realignments in the leagues were frequent as school sizes changed, and new, well-matched, and conven-

IRVING S. "NIG" ROSE (7 Feb. 1893–6 Aug. 1972) was treasurer of the Cleveland Baseball Federation for over 50 years. He helped raise over $1 million to finance sandlot baseball in Cleveland by promoting the annual Sandlot Day exhibition baseball game played by the Cleveland Indians. Rose also took the lead in forming the Cleveland Municipal Softball Association, which adopted rules to streamline the game and make it more exciting for spectators. An employee and close associate of clothier Max Rosenblum, he managed the Cleveland Rosenblums of the American Basketball League; the team won 3 championships in the 1920s.

iently located competitors were sought. No longer were scholastic athletics in Cleveland divided into simple east and west divisions.

By the late 1980s Cleveland was being hailed as a "comeback city." It had emerged from default and, by virtue of a major promotion launched by the Greater Cleveland Growth Association's New Cleveland Campaign, garnered national at-

Nig Rose accepts checks from "sandlotters" Rich Rollins and Oakland A's catcher Sal Bando for the Cleveland Baseball Federation, 12 June 1970. *Cleveland Press Collection, Cleveland State University.*

tention. In attempting to attract businesses and residents, this and other programs (and perhaps the passage of time and the dulling of memories) successfully dispelled the negative images of riots, burning rivers, and rusted factories, and promoted the city's cultural amenities and business advantages. A large part of such national promotions of the city centered around sports. Cleveland was a big-league city, and its professional teams, especially the Browns, were touted as a civic asset.

Cleveland also had advantages for the individual sportsman. Many of the glossy promotional brochures aimed at attracting new residents to the area pictured golf courses, tennis courts, and boating. Indeed, boating, which had once been the sole purview of the wealthy, had now become widespread. First conducted as an

Running has its moment in the sun in Cleveland as the field of competitors moves past the starting line at the 1991 Revco Marathon. Edward Howard Company; Stephen Crompton Photography.

By the late 1930s, baseball and softball teams competed in leagues under administration by the Cleveland Baseball Federation and the Cleveland Municipal Softball Association. Shown here is the Clark Recreation team, city champs in 1938–39. Cleveland Press Collection, Cleveland State University.

FRANCES SOBCZAK KASZUBSKI (25 May 1916–   ) is a former amateur athlete and has been an advocate of women's sports programs. She was the United States champion in shot put and discus 19 times from 1933 to 1952 and received a bronze medal in the discus at the first Pan-American Games, held in 1951. A fine basketball player, Kaszubski was named national AAU center in 1943. From 1948 to 1960, she was instrumental in bringing together warring national sports organizations. Her efforts in eliciting cooperation among various associations of women's physical education teachers, the Amateur Athletic Union (AAU), and the United States Olympic Committee led to the development of varsity sports programs for girls in secondary schools and colleges.

organized local "sport" with the formation of the Cleveland Yacht Club in 1878, boat ownership exploded in the 1970s and 1980s. Over 30,000 boats were registered in Cuyahoga County in 1986. Not many of the new boating aficionados, however,

Olympian Frances Kaszubski throws the discus at the AAU Women's Track and Field Championships at Waterbury, Connecticut, in August 1951. *Cleveland Public Library.*

used their craft for racing and regattas, as had been the case in the pre–World War II era. Often powered by motors and requiring little muscle or skill to operate, the boats were pleasure craft for weekend get-aways and relaxation. More likely than not, Cleveland boaters wanted to sail the Cuyahoga River and tie up at one of the many bars now lining that waterway. Whereas in the 1850s, industry had forced the rowers of the Ivanhoe Boat Club off the river, in the 1980s, recreational use of the river presented nightmares for ore freighter captains trying to get their cargoes to the city's few remaining steel plants.

Cleveland, however, may not have entered a true renaissance in the 1980s. The emphasis on downtown development masked the continuing deterioration of the city's neighborhoods, all but one of which lost population during the decade. The loss of manufacturing jobs left a significant portion of the unskilled in the city's population with little employment outside of that in the service economy, which often paid little more than minimum wage. A review of the city's structural and economic problems might also reveal that the postwar parallel between the fate of the city and its sports teams was, indeed, very real. While suburban sports prospered, those in the city suffered continued decline. Not only were the public schools not producing many championship teams, but city parks and playgrounds were heavily vandalized and, in many cases, served as the sites for illegal drug deals. Moreover, drugs in professional sports provided an all-too-frightening parallel, and perhaps even a model, for what was happening in the city. The revelation in 1983–84 that several Cleveland Browns players were being treated for cocaine addiction was only the beginning of the tragic story. The death of Browns defensive back Don Rogers in 1986 from cocaine use showed that the problem had not been solved. Later in the decade, a new star fullback for the Browns would find himself in drug-related trouble. At the end of the decade, the discovery of the coach of the Cleveland State University basketball team in a local crackhouse, and his subsequent confession of excessive use of alcohol and drugs, created major problems for the CSU basketball team—at that time the city's only team playing in a major collegiate circuit. The CSU Vikings had both a winning record and a reputation for providing opportunity for students coming out of the inner city. The coach's involvement with drugs as well as an earlier recruiting scandal tarnished the team's image.

Coupled with the issue of drug use by professional athletes were the soaring

The regal sport of yachting adapted easily to Cleveland's many rivers and Lake Erie. The yacht pictured here is departing from Rocky River in 1935. *Western Reserve Historical Society.*

Social Mirror, Economic Engine, and Civic Asset

MARK H. McCORMACK (6 Nov. 1930–   ), Cleveland lawyer and sports agent, is the primary force behind the International Management Group, the pioneering firm in the promotion of athletes and sporting events. McCormack attended Yale University Law School and served in the army before joining the firm of Arter & Hadden. He established IMG in 1959. In the 1960s McCormack became the agent for golfers Arnold Palmer, Gary Player, and Jack Nicklaus. In 1991 the agency had worldwide offices and produced hundreds of millions in revenues annually through sports representation and entertainment productions.

salaries in the professional game, a phenomenon which some argued set another bad example for local youth. Where sports had once denoted teamwork, sacrifice, and ability, they were now viewed by many as an avenue to easy riches, wherein drug use, college cheating, and academic failure would be tolerated if one's "game" was good enough. The most telling sign about Cleveland's comeback was the fact that while more than once Cleveland teams made it to the playoffs, they never achieved the final goal—winning a championship.

On the more positive side for both the city and its teams, responsible athletes helped to counter these negative images by investing their time and money in visiting schools to lecture against drug and alcohol abuse and by running athletic skills training classes at Cuyahoga Community College and local high schools. Others worked with the Police Athletic League, the local branch of which had been founded in 1956, in trying to channel the energies of Cleveland's urban youth into competitive sporting activities such as boxing, bowling, and football. These athletes, along with the police, realized quite clearly that in 1980s America and Cleveland, there was no more potent role model for youth than a successful athlete. While Coveleski, Kuhel, and Vosmik had been the images of success for the children of Cleveland's white immigrants, Jim Chones and Lenny Wilkens of the Cavaliers, and Ozzie Newsom of the Browns, along with a score of black athletes, became the models for the city's African-American children in the 1980s.

By the 1980s, not only were sports popular in Cleveland, but playing games had become integral to the area's economy. Sports were no longer a leisure-time luxury but a business of vast economic worth to the area. By mid-decade, the Cleveland Browns were valued at $50 million, the Indians at $35 million, and the Cavaliers at $15 million. Residents in the metropolitan Cleveland area spent over $1 billion annually on sports. The extent and importance of sport's generated monies were best represented by the worldwide growth of Mark H. McCormack's Cleveland-based International Management Group. Begun in 1960 when McCormack, a Cleveland lawyer, became the business agent for golfer Arnold Palmer, IMG had over 500 clients by the mid-1980s and brought in annual revenues of $300 million— this represented only IMG's profit on the huge sums it managed for both athletes and athletic events. With such sums of money tied up in the sports sector, it was obviously important for the city to keep both the owners and the fans of local sports teams happy. By the mid-1980s, some civic leaders were convinced that this meant building a new stadium.

Mark H. McCormack, founder of International Management Group, one of the world's premier sports representation agencies. *International Management Group.*

Sports camps have been highly successful in training both the minds and bodies of Cleveland's inner-city youth. Here Tracy Hall of Cleveland Heights, an All-American at Ohio State, instructs young participants at a Cuyahoga Community College camp. *Cuyahoga Community College.*

Despite extensive repairs to the Municipal Stadium, including an $8 million renovation undertaken by Art Modell after he secured a twenty-five-year lease on the facility in 1974, many in Cleveland hankered for something newer and grander. Domed facilities had been the rage ever since the Astrodome opened in Houston in 1965. Climate-controlled and equipped with private loges—which businesses could use to entertain important clients—these modern coliseums were monuments to the impact on American life of professional sports. To be up-to-date and competitive, claimed civic boosters across the country, a city needed a domed stadium. A move to construct such a facility in Cleveland was begun in 1986 with the formation of the Domed Stadium Corporation. However, by 1989, it was clear that this private initiative would not succeed. Eventually the project came under partial control of the county and city governments. By 1990, plans had changed—a domed

The present-day site of the Gateway Project occupies what was once Cleveland's Central Market district along Ontario Street. *Western Reserve Historical Society.*

The GATEWAY ECONOMIC DEVELOPMENT CORPORATION OF GREATER CLEVELAND, a private nonprofit organization, was created jointly by Cleveland and Cuyahoga County to administrate construction of Cleveland's proposed new stadium and arena. Completion of the $349 million project, located on the 28-acre Old Central Market site downtown, was targeted for spring 1994. The open-air natural-grass ballpark will be the new home of the Cleveland Indians, seating 45,000 spectators while being capable of expanding to 72,000 for football games. The NBA Cleveland Cavaliers are to occupy the 20,000-seat sports and entertainment arena.

facility was no longer on the drawing board. Instead, backers, including businessmen and government officials, proposed the construction of a sports and hotel complex that would include a smaller baseball-oriented stadium and a new in-town arena for basketball and other sports. Underwritten in part by a new tax on alcohol and tobacco approved by county voters after an intensive campaign including television appeals by the city's mayor, and by the publicly approved sale of revenue bonds, this sports center project, christened "Gateway," was viewed in 1990 as a key to Cleveland's future growth and prosperity. In perhaps the ultimate historic irony, the facility was slated to be built in the area that had housed the city's market and wholesale houses since the 1820s. Where once Clevelanders had bought and sold the very necessities of life, their descendants would cheer the athletes of the twenty-first

A detailed artist's rendering of Gateway Stadium looking north to downtown, with the Arena in the background. *Gateway Economic Development Corporation.*

century and, in doing so, perhaps be as central to the regional economy as the farmers and traders of the 1800s.

Whether many Clevelanders perceived this irony is an open question, for Gateway was the result of a historical process that came to a rapid culmination in the years after 1945. Remembering only what they had experienced, many younger Clevelanders could not envision a time when sports had not been important, and even for their parents and grandparents, who may have been born as early as 1900, sports were an integral part of their experience. That games were once a luxury in Cleveland is a fact that predates living memory. That games are now viewed as an economic and civic necessity is also a fact, and one that would have been unfathomable to those who first settled on the banks of the Cuyahoga River some two hundred years ago.

Note: All photo references are in *bold italics.*